Praise for
GOD ON THE ROCKS

"Thank God for a storyteller like Phil Madeira, who delivers a feast for the ears, and for the mind, as he ponders the traditions of his family and the mysteries of the faith that have shaped his life. Like every good thing in life, it was over too soon."

—Amy Grant

"GOD ON THE ROCKS is an amazing heart-of-the-music-business journey that puts the reader on a path of discovery that leads to a vulnerable encounter with the God of beauty. Madeira writes in a sharp, funny style and never strikes a false note."

—Frank Schaeffer, author of *Crazy for God*

"If you're a cage-pacing, God-haunted pilgrim like me, then this deftly penned collection of stories will deeply move you. Madeira's voice is gritty and tender, broody and vulnerable, unwaveringly honest, yet compassionate. I'm supremely grateful for this heartfelt travelogue of faith."

—Ian Morgan Cron, bestselling author of *Jesus, My Father, The CIA, and Me: A Memoir...of Sorts*, and *Chasing Francis: A Pilgrim's Tale*

"This gritty, gutsy, funny, moving, insightful spiritual memoir not only introduces a gifted writer (who also happens to be a stellar musician), but it also exemplifies a growing phenomenon on the American religious landscape, an emerging spiritual ethos that defies standard labels and has the feel of our best roots music."

—Brian D. McLaren, author / speaker (www.brianmclaren.net)

"Phil shows us how faith is often born in simple yet sacred experiences and can be rediscovered in our willingness to remember."

—Jennifer Knapp

"Whether he's driving us down Route 114 to Barrington, Rhode Island, 'to drink the punch made of that evangelical staple—ginger ale,' or leading us up South Cove Trail at Radnor Lake in Nashville to commune with God 'where purple wild flowers are draped like royal robes across a shaded meadow,' Phil dares to reveals his scars—and the wound's still open. But beyond the hurt and the healing, his faith is unrelenting and hope prevails. It's a soul-stirring journey to undergo, especially with a genuine poet such as Phil Madeira as your guide."

—Steve Hindalong

GOD
ON THE
ROCKS

Distilling Religion, Savoring Faith

PHIL MADEIRA

JERICHO
BOOKS™

New York • Boston • Nashville

Jericho Books
Hachette Book Group
237 Park Avenue
New York, NY 10017

www.JerichoBooks.com

The author is represented by Creative Trust, Inc.

Printed in the United States of America

RRD-C

First edition July 2013
10 9 8 7 6 5 4 3 2 1

Jericho Books is an imprint of Hachette Book Group, Inc..
The Jericho Books name and logo are trademarks of Hachette Book Group, Inc.

The Hachette Speakers Bureau provides a wide range of authors for speaking events. To find out more, go to www.HachetteSpeakersBureau.com or call (866) 376-6591.

The publisher is not responsible for websites (or their content) that are not owned by the publisher.

Library of Congress Control Number: 2013903917

To Kate, Maddy, and my Southern Born Woman

Contents

God on the Rocks

1

Beat Generation

I am the baby who tumbled from the womb drumming. I am the boy whose fingers tapped out a tattoo on a maple-topped desk in elementary school. I am the teenager who split the calfskin head of an old Ludwig drum as my blue-and-gold-clad fellows marched ahead, laden down with cumbersome brass tubas and silver cornets.

Be it a Sunday school class or a marching band, a book group or an English Lit class, I've never been swept along with the herd. I might be singing along to whatever melody is being raised by the chorus, but the tempo in my head is always fighting with the cadence of the footfalls of the communal parade.

The rhythm in my head is upbeat and funky. The snare drum barks with brassy insistence and the bass drum holds it all together, landing solidly on the beat, while a maraca trips erratically overhead, riding on the wind.

And the beat goes on.

Those who love me have sometimes felt the need to explain or excuse me. My childhood shenanigans would often elicit an exclamation of "Where did you come from?" from my bemused father. Exasperated, my mother would plead with me to get in line with dress codes, mores, or whatever parental vision I was supposed to be fulfilling.

It's no wonder that I'm marching to my own beat. My parents set me up.

While I was incubating in my mother's tummy, she was playing Mahalia Jackson records, feeding my soul the music of a world that was vastly different from white -bread New England. The gift of my mother's beloved black gospel music was the siren's call, the sound that lured my vessel away from the staid New England harbor only to joyously capsize me on the jagged edges of rock 'n' roll.

When she preached on Mother's Day, it was to a congregation who wasn't sure what to do with the idea of a woman having that kind of authority. She was more progressive than she knew. She didn't know she was a rebel; but sometimes taking the words of Jesus at face value can start a revolution.

My father, a man's man if I ever knew one, was somewhat of a pacifist, bringing yet another strange facet into an otherwise dog-eat-dog world. He presided over the Rhode Island chapter of Habitat for Humanity, and he created a relief society to benefit destitute people in Haiti.

Dad was a minister in a Baptist church, known more for what they don't do than for what they get done. Yet, unlike many Baptists, he preached less about Hell than of the Church's responsibility to the poor. He ruffled the feathers of his flock when he preached against the war in Vietnam, and when he championed men like Martin Luther King, Jr.

My parents' literal interpretation of the words of Christ made them who they were. They took faith seriously, and thus set themselves apart from the self-centered suburbia they lived in. They were truly "in the world, but not of the world."

My parents were proudly Evangelical, espousing a holistic gospel both theologically pronounced and practiced.

There were many churches in waspy Barrington, the upper-class town we lived in. Although Rhode Island was founded by the first

Baptist, Roger Williams, being Baptist carried with it a hillbilly stigma among the bluebloods of New England. The social climbers attended St. John's Episcopal or the White Church, an aptly named Congregational group on the banks of the Barrington River.

There were two Catholic churches, one Methodist, another less-well-heeled Episcopal parish, and a synagogue just to round things out.

My parents would answer my questions about what the other churches believed with phrases that caused me to think that we at Barrington Baptist had quite a bit more truth than the rest of the town's Christians. "Well, they don't really know the Lord the way we do" was the gist of it. It was always something of a surprise for me to find out that an Episcopalian or a Congregationalist could be a "real Christian."

In their quest to espouse a religion that matched up with who they believed Jesus to be, they were more exclusive than they may have realized. That is the difficulty with most denominations.

My life was designed by my parents to revolve around church events several days a week. Sunday was filled with Sunday school class, morning worship, afternoon youth group, and evening worship. There was also Wednesday evening prayer meeting, which I was thankful that we were not required to attend, and Friday night youth activities in the church gymnasium.

By the time I was eighteen years old, I had done enough church-going to fill the average lifetime.

When I left the warmth of my parents' home for my freshman year of college, I sought out other Christians like them, but there were none that I could find. At Taylor University, I recognized the religious jargon, and found some comfort in being with "real Christians," but there was something missing.

I attended chapel services and occasionally went to one church or another on Sunday, but sleeping in seemed a more constructive op-

tion. I let myself off the hook based on my behavior and "time served."
I still do.

Over the years, the search for God's presence led me in and out of a
variety of traditions, from incense burners to barn burners, liturgists
to improvisers. In contrast to conventional church wisdom, the more
active I became in one group or another, the less connected to Christ I
felt.

What my parents loved to experience with many, I cherish with one
or two people, and more so under the low lighting of a bar than the
brightly lit chandeliers of a church sanctuary.

Trying to remain a good parent to the end, my nonagenarian
mother still sends me books by prominent Evangelical authors. I'm in
good company, mind you; she sends devotional books to the president
of the United States! Once, after reading something Barack Obama
had said about his spiritual life, Mom told me that she was quite sure
he had read the book she'd sent him. If that's the case, he's one up on
me.

Unfortunately, what was once meaningful jargon now falls flat
when it hits my ears. I can't read these books. It's hard enough for me
to read the Bible, so familiar is it to me. But the language of Evangelicalism seems like a pair of loaded dice; I know exactly where the roll
will take me. I need something fresh.

Surprise me, God.

Once I tried to explain to my mother that I was grateful for my
upbringing in the household of faith, but no longer felt comfortable defining myself as Evangelical. She voiced her disappointment by
projecting it through my father, long deceased, saying, "Yah fathuh
would be mighty disappointed in you. He was proud to be Evangelical."

Ah, yes, Mom will always play the Dad card. But it never works;
it stings for a moment, but it's never a surprise. It's a Band-Aid being
pulled off, nothing more. Dad never worried about the drumbeat I

was following. Mom feels bad that I'm not in the club anymore no matter how much I explain that I am still trying to follow Christ.

What I don't say, but perhaps she understands, is that I can't seem to find Jesus in that world that loudly proclaims him. The fever pitch of the crowd makes it hard for me to hear what the Old Testament calls "the still, small voice." The rants of the church are about hanging on to theological and social real estate, while the whisper of the Spirit is "Let go."

I'm doing my best to let go, by God.

I try to give my mother some comfort in the idea that she is largely responsible for my exit from Evangelical World; after all, she never let the word "Baptist" define her parameters, never caved to the status quo when it would have been convenient. She was a pastor's wife who didn't limit herself to playing the piano on Sunday mornings. The open-minded attitude she had as a young woman probably had more influence on my father's ministry than anything else. They were a team, trying to live out the words of Christ.

I'm their son, trying to live *in* the words of Christ.

While I am trying to escape the sound of her voice, I try to silence it by reminding her that her affection for her Lutheran upbringing, with its liturgical trappings, paved the way for me to find life in the closely related Episcopal tradition. I like the ancient prayers, concise and reflective, and empty of ego and emotion, unlike the risky extemporaneous offerings of some long-winded preachers I've known.

But despite my explanations and arguments, I think she is left to wonder if her son is what she used to call "a real Christian." Why couldn't I have just tuned out that damned drumbeat, and blended in?

A friend asked me once if I could go back to my hometown and life in the world I knew as a young man. He already knew the answer. Thomas Wolfe said it best: "You can't go home again." Indeed, the place of my beginning is dear to me, but it is only a faint replica of *Home*.

Home is what I hope my children sense when my arms are around them. It is a place I see in my Dearest Companion's eyes. It is the vibration of a lone guitar, tuned to an open D, resonating with the room it sits in. Home is the unmistakable pattern of two drumsticks on a calfskin head; it is the humming that accompanies pilgrimage.

2

Southern by the Grace of God

My mother always noted that I was born in New Hampshire, and that for the first two years of my life, my home was in a hamlet dreadfully named Gonic, where my father was the sparsely rewarded minister of the Baptist church. It always annoyed me to know that I was born in their worst years, as if I had tumbled out of her womb with an IOU slip pinned to my big toe. A boy likes to know that he brought bounty with him, good luck, or prosperity, but I just brought rhythm. Born drumming, she still says.

Those were the meager years of their lives, even worse than when Dad was a circuit rider in Maine, dividing his sermons between three churches in the rocky farmland far from any semblance of coastal romance. Before God Almighty moved our family to Rhode Island, Dad preached to callous-handed farmers and laborers who tithed with bushels of corn or apples, or with their skills, perhaps fixing the parsonage's eternally running toilet, or unloading a cord of firewood.

My mother relishes those days of depending on God's provision, likening their time in the Granite State to the prophet Elijah's stint in the wilderness, as if we were eating raven flesh and locusts instead of Cream of Wheat. She possesses the admirable trait of being nonmaterialistic, and is thus warmed by thoughts of waiting on God Almighty to prove himself in the days of simple needs.

For years, she has repeated stories of God's mercy in those days of waiting on the Almighty. One morning, she says, she and my father were singing praises when a twenty-dollar bill appeared, hidden within their hymnal's pages for who knows how long, until just the right moment.

Another time, knowing a fierce Maine winter was approaching, my mother privately prayed for a warm coat. Soon, a parishioner turned up with a bolt of wool, which someone else sewed into the sorely needed garment.

My mother glories in those days of high snow and low dough.

I have no such sentiments about New Hampshire or the North.

Not long ago, when we had a rare conversation, she said, "You've lost yaw New England accent." This was music to my ears, because I like to pretend that I never talked like a Yankee. I still cling to one mispronunciation that my Southern Born Woman teases me for using—"aftawoods," a single clue to my northern raising.

You see, my body may have been born in New Hampshire, but my soul was born in South Carolina. I'm sure of it. My mother used to tell me how she and Dad and I drove from New England to South Carolina. Dad had been invited to preach at a church in the low country, whose congregation needed a shepherd. I can't remember if an invitation to take the job followed the audition, but we went instead to Rhode Island, where he and Mom lived until his Alzheimer's disease led them to Connecticut, but that's another story.

My siblings were left with their maternal grandmother in Cranston, Rhode Island, but my parents chose to bring their little eighteen-month-old son on their pilgrimage. I was given the entire backseat of their old '49 Ford, with, naturally, no seatbelts, restraints, or infant seat. As my parents sat in the front, probably discussing their uncertain future, I quietly and methodically threw every last toy I owned out the window, watching them disappear behind us on a hot

Carolina highway. In those rare conversations with my mother, I'm told I was an expensive child.

Somewhere in South Carolina, Dad pulled the car into a rest area, and let it cool under the hickory tree that sheltered a lone picnic table. As they unpacked their basket and blanket, an old black man and his daughter ambled up to the car. Before my mother could spread her tablecloth across the table, the man's daughter staked her claim to it by laying her large torso across it. Thus, my mother invited the two to partake of our simple meal.

There's not much to the story, although it reminds me of my parents' high regard for "Negroes," as Mom called them. She loved this story because, in the end, the old man took me in his arms and held me for the duration of their lunch. She said he was "wonduhful."

And that's where my story, or whatever it is, begins. It has to start someplace, and New Hampshire has never worked for me, as the Granite State has no ties to the moaning melodies and sensual, shuffling rhythms that I can't shake. The blues record spinning at thirty-three and a third in my soul could never be titled "New Hampshire Blues."

It must be a common question: "Who am I?"

Perhaps the answer is found in the question "Who is God?"

In the meantime, reinvention is a common theme among pilgrims who are trying to make sense of the pilgrimage. We struggle to make meaning for and of ourselves, hoofing it along the stony, serpentine path of this short life. We look beyond blood and heritage, religion and science, and find ourselves reflected in *Other*. Some of us simultaneously look for a group to belong to, and a group to be free of.

Maybe it's magical thinking, maybe I'm just a blue-collar mystic, but I'm fixated on the idea of God Almighty whispering a Muddy Waters tune into my soul, his ancient whiskers scratching my infant skin, both disturbing me and tickling me, and leaving me with the inescapable yearn to hum over a seventh chord.

Who was that old man, that son of slaves, with his sweet smile and low hum? I wonder if he secretly made some sign on my brow, or spoke some ancient word into my ear, and perhaps sang some old gospel melody as he held on to me. Whatever the case, I always knew that I was a southern man with a bluesman's heart, long before I finally packed up and moved to Dixieland. My name is Philip, and I'm from South Carolina.

3

Passageway

Gravity pulls me toward Dad, and then away from him.

I'm picturing myself standing in the middle of the bench seat of Dad's old '55 Ford, with a hand on Dad's shoulder as he negotiates an S curve on The Trail. David is to my right, and we are cheering like banshees as Dad accelerates. We lean hard left and hard right, as Dad counts by tens, "Seventy...eighty...ninety...."

Seatbelts were optional, and Dad was admirably frugal, and as he took the turquoise-and-cream-colored Ford 500 up to one hundred miles per hour, we knew we were living large. Not for a moment did we imagine that Dad was reckless; in truth, I don't think he was much of a risk-taker. I don't know if he'd go five miles an hour above the limit with Mom in the car, but when it was just Dad and the boys, we were born to be wild.

"Just how wild?" you ask.

Some fathers give their sons their first drink, while others employ them in the family business. I've heard of despicable fathers introducing their sons to the local brothel. Well, our dad didn't do any of those things. But what he did do was teach us that it was fine to be whoever we were. And as we sailed down that curvy strip of road, we celebrated being men. The windows were down, the salty air was messing up our hair, and the old man was grinning to beat the band.

United by blood, by name, and by the New York Yankees, we had a bond that remains, even though Dad is long gone. I can't tell you what he did do insure the survival of our fellowship, but I think it has to do with his beaming eyes, pure smile, and unconditional love for his boys.

Tearing up the asphalt with us at his side, he didn't know we'd become hippies in the seventies, or Episcopalians in the nineties. He didn't know we'd fail in our marriages, or swear like sailors, which wouldn't have brought him any great joy. I think he dreamed for his sons to be exactly as he allowed them to be in those days of innocence: themselves.

Granted, we redefined ourselves in ways that might have confounded him, but he never lost the ability to celebrate his boys and our bond with him. Our troubles and misadventures were never enough for him to throw in the towel. The long hair and beards and the enthusiasm for counterculture music didn't put Dad off or cause him the kind of anxiety that crippled other parents of our generation.

While Dad didn't speak like a Zen master, perhaps his faith was so informed that he could embrace the journey each of us was on, believing that everything has its place in a life—the failure, the victory, the weeds, and the roses.

The Wampanoag Trail, or "The Trail" as locals call it, is a winding piece of road that connects my hometown of Barrington with the interstate highway system and thus to the rest of America. A decade later, I'd be leaning my own Ford into the same exhilarating Ss, not worrying about the 45-mph speed limit. Decades later, with daughters safely strapped into an older Mercedes station wagon, I'd be doing the same thing, but a diesel doesn't deliver the same thrill as does high-octane gasoline coursing through a mammoth V8.

Madeira men have always had a thing for cars. We have a soft spot for Fords, just like the ones Dad drove, and like the '63 Ford Falcon we learned on. Once a year, I'll find myself perusing online auction sites for a Falcon Country Squire station wagon, as if the nostalgic euphoria will outweigh the comfort of modernity.

The Trail is the last landmark on a long journey from Nashville to Barrington. There aren't many markers over the course of a thousand miles, and apart from the giant guitar in Bristol, Tennessee, most of them come within the last two hundred miles of the journey — the Tappan Zee Bridge, the "Welcome to Rhode Island" sign, a giant termite in Providence, and finally a small sign saying "Route 114 to Barrington."

Mile markers, signposts, and landmarks all remind us of one thing: *We aren't there yet.*

I've also heard it said, *You can never go back.*

Ergo, we aren't there yet, and we can never go back.

Dad is a symbol of what I might aspire to be, a good father, a decent person, fair, honest, kind, and considerate. Yet, when I visit Barrington, the place where I first knew him, I am always disappointed by the changes in landscape, the new supermarkets, the Walgreens, and the Starbucks. Like my old Falcon, gone are the mom 'n' pop joints — barbershops and drugstores, diners and garages — with few exceptions.

I can picture my father with a Starbucks cup in his hand about as easily as I can picture my mother holding a cat. It doesn't compute. Dad frequented the simple, working-class eateries, brought his Fords to a shade-tree mechanic, and shopped for groceries at the A&P, which closed shop long before Dad's mind did.

These changes remind me that one can't go back. My daughters and I drive past an overgrown lot, and I'll point to what appears to be nothing, and say, "That's where West Barrington Elementary School used to be. That's where Uncle Dave and I went to grade school."

Impressive.

We pass my parents' home on Salisbury Road, which is so much smaller than I remember, its formerly green sides having been painted a muted magenta. It looks *something* like our old house. If we were invited in, the smell of cardamom bread would be long gone, and I'm sure the kitchen linoleum would finally have been replaced, but that little house was really all about what books were on the shelves and what photos and paintings hung on the walls. It was about the sound of a voice saying "Love ya, Mom!" on its way to school. The sound of Dad's "amen" when the blessing had been said. The aroma of clam chowder sitting on a warm stove.

One of the few things that makes sense is the Barrington Cemetery, where we search for Dad's grave, remembering only that it is toward the back of the graveyard. It's a place where we mark no change, apart from the pebbles left on his stone, or the wilted flowers left by a well-wisher. "Nothing's changed" is an ironic illusion for those of us who want to grow, stretch, and mature into the person we feel called to be.

For a man who wants to change, it is ironic that I want to go back. The eradication of *the way things were* saddens me, along with the erosion of an era, and the fading echoes of what should be memorable. We go back to these places to find ourselves, and we're not there.

The pilgrimage of humanity is to orbit a mirage resembling "home." All but the most cynical of us feel the pull between worlds, the gravity of the way it was and is juxtaposed with the weightlessness of dreams and a longing for what some of us call God.

The place that we are in is not a place, but in the passageway between places. We're in the journey, and blessed if we sense the companionship of God's spirit. Perhaps when we see glimpses of God along the way, we are finding ourselves as well.

4

The Grandmonster

I was all of four years old, milling about my curtained and dark bedroom, while listening to my playmates exult outside on a summer day. Those familiar primeval melodies that must have echoed back and forth between Cain and Abel drifted from the street and between the slatted blinds my grandmother had so deliberately shut.

My mother's mother was babysitting for me, and in her wisdom, she believed a boy needed a nap. It didn't matter to her that I was simply not going to drift off into the Land of Nod. It was the way things were to be.

I still remember the exact spot in which I stood, opening a bureau drawer as the bedroom door swung open. She looked like a giant to me, backlit by the hall light, her white hair lit by a halo hardly befitting this nonangelic intruder.

Her annoyed tone carried a song of shame. Her English was void of ws, quaintly endearing to some, but grating to me.

"Vhy aren't you sleeping!?" she trumpeted. "I wish you'd go to Hell!" I burst out, knowing Hell was the Bad Place, but not realizing that "go to Hell" was a less than quaint colloquialism.

Apart from a recollection of my uncle Gene putting an ice cube down my two-year-old back, this is my first memory, quaint and endearing indeed.

What followed my outburst remains provocatively forgotten. I doubt that I escaped unscathed, and I assume my punishment was so severe that I've blocked it for all these many years. Of course, I deserved something for my unrestrained and bitter words. In all likelihood, she washed my mouth out with Ivory Soap, appropriate for the crime and acceptable for the times. And when my mother returned, no doubt I was held on her lap and my posterior regions laid into with the right hand of the law.

I wasn't diplomatic enough to explain to my grandmonster that my mother was perfectly happy to let me expend every ounce of energy I had on a summer day, or that the ancient melodies wafting up from the street were calling to my primeval heart, and that it was impossible to ward off the sirens' taunts. Diplomacy aside, there was no convincing this immovable Swede.

This incident has been part of our family mythology for many years now, highlighting my audaciousness—a four-year-old telling his grandma where to go.

She didn't go there soon enough, however, and until she grew senile in her nineties, she was present to disapprove of nearly everything I did.

For the span of thirty-six years, and then some, "Mormor" was very plain about the disturbance I was in her life. There was nothing I could do to please this woman. She would often ask me, in exasperation, "Vhy can't you be like David and Ann-Elise?" my older siblings. I used to scratch my head, wondering what I'd done to deserve her consistent chiding, but I could never quite figure it out.

"Vhy can't you do things the right vay?" "Vat do you think Yeesus thinks of you?" and "If your father knew the vay you behaved, he'd spank you good" were all verses in her soulless liturgy.

She believed that I played the drums just to annoy my mother. I remember her coming down to the basement where I played, flipping the light switch on and off, frantically trying to get my attention, a look of utter panic having overtaken her face, finally cupping her hands over her ears. I'm sure she believed that I had been taken over by some demonic force, and that these syncopated rhythms I played were straight out of Satan's forbidden jungle.

Indeed, I was transfixed by rhythm and soul and the visceral nature of rock 'n' roll.

That my bluesboy heart could hope for understanding from this woman whose feet were rooted in frozen, unyielding Swedish soil now seems quite unreasonable. However, it's a fair to expect one's grandmother to love her grandchild. *she DID - Tried to warn!*

Thus, I played harder and louder. (I confess to testing the ties that bind.)

Once, I remember sitting around our dining room table, Mormor, Dad, a girlfriend, and me. Mom was away visiting Sweden, and Dad felt the obligation to do something nice for his mother-in-law, which meant doing something not-so-nice for me. Thinking he might give her a reason to appreciate me, Dad suggested, "Phil, why don't you play 'O Sacred Head, Now Wounded' for Mormor?"

I was a college student, and had taken a semester of piano, hoping to discipline my wild fingers by learning a Bach piece. I had happily memorized a fugue and the moving Bach hymn "O Sacred Head."

"He'd only ruin it," she assured the stunned room.

I've never played it since.

Music, a common thread running through the tapestries of both my parents' families, was something that my grandmother believed I was defiling. I think she had genuine concern for my soul and bewilderment for how to rescue me, but her grand error was believing that the attempt to control me was the solution. If anything solidified my insistence on clinging to who I wanted to be and steering my ship to a destination of my choosing, it was my mother and grandmother's desire to take the tiller out of my hands. *(rebellion)*

We never found our common ground, and any attempts on her part

in obedience to what spirit!!!

to be pleasant were usually thinly masked strategies to make me acceptable. She even wrote me a letter when I was in college, kindly suggesting that I would be so much happier if I would give my heart to a more civilized expression than rock 'n' roll. Yet, as my story reveals, the thought of my attempting to play a Bach hymn was akin to sacrilege to her. It was shameful to her that she had a blasphemer for a grandson. *b/c it grieved her Lord.*

If only I had been born and baptized on a Sunday.

So, what of my profane declaration to my mother's mother? Some people find this story peculiar and disturbing, while I see it as a gasp for air, a demand for recognition. *←yes. Self.*

I don't want to bask in the warmth of my rudeness, but it probably saved me from going in a direction that *(the world)* life never intended for me. Years later, my father told me I should be grateful for his mother-in-law's inability to accept me for who I was, believing that she taught me early on that you'll never be satisfied if you follow anyone else's call but your own.

oops! You DO need to follow God's call.

5

Beads

A voice is full of possibility. A voice can gently call you to rise and take on the day, or cruelly remind you that you've awakened to an unkind reality. A voice can sing you to sleep, or call you to arms. It can tell you the truth or sell you a lie.

A voice, even my own voice, will ruin my heart, if I listen to it too much. Better to burn it with a dram of whisky, and catch the ill word in the back of my throat before I send a verbal boomerang into the void.

One's inner voice can do plenty of damage, too. The voice that whispers failure, misery, depression, doom is difficult to silence.

Thus, one seeks the voice that can trump all others. The babbling brook. The howling wind. The shouting thunder. The whispering dewdrops on green petals.

I walk at a local nature reserve called Radnor Lake, where I enjoy the subtle changes the seasons bring. I walk there year-round, often with my Dearest Companion, my Southern Born Woman, who, unlike me, can tell one tree from another. She, whose soul is keenly aware that the voice of God has many shapes, songs, and sounds, makes for a perfect companion in this undulating, breathing cathedral.

One spectacular spring evening, she and I were on the east side of the lake watching the sun set, when some natural phenomenon occurred and a cross appeared inside a circle formed by the sun. We notice these things, she and I, wondering at creation's constant declaration of glory. These moments can make you feel infinitesimally small or startlingly significant.

In early spring, I like looking down from high on the ridge, where all manner of green things are sprouting. The forest has yet to become thick with growth, so one can look far into the woods, as the liveliest hues of green scatter joy across its floor.

With the approach of Holy Week, the wildflowers spread a majestic purple carpet deep in the woods, and thoughts of the Resurrection drift into my consciousness, reminding me of the Impossible Things my heart believes in.

In May, new fawns are getting used to their spindly legs. By June, they're nearly eating out of your hand, which, of course, they shouldn't do; there are all kinds of signs saying "Don't Touch the Deer," but in a much more verbose fashion, giving scientific explanations for why you'll kill them if you touch them. A bit dramatic, but I suppose it works.

My Southern Born Woman and I enjoy our June walks at Radnor, noting the many turtles sunning themselves on protruding logs, wondering how they climbed to their perches, and chuckling when we hear the splash of one dropping back into the cool water. The Canada geese are plentiful, and occasionally we see a heron, moving stoically and deliberately, waiting for an unsuspecting fish.

Early one June evening, as we were coming to the end of our walk, we noticed a silent and still owl sitting on a branch near the edge of the woods, as if to acknowledge two pilgrims at a journey's end. I've never thought much about owls till recently, and it was this dusk sighting that intrigued me, so intent was her stare as we gazed upon her.

Owls move silently and swiftly. There is no rustling of feathers as they spirit themselves about the nocturnal world. Their night vision is Sheffield sharp, and nothing is hidden from them. As she looked at us, I wondered if she was looking into us.

By July, the lake is covered with a thick coat of green algae, and the wildlife has disappeared from view. A rank stink rises from the lake, and it's clear that summer is here to stay.

Eventually, autumn leaves are falling, and the crisp air returns, and the trees cut stark silhouettes against the November sky. And thus it remains until spring breaks her silence and yawns.

And so on.

Sometimes I walk alone.

My hike comprises two essential loops, first the lofty and solitary South Cove Trail, and then the low-country Lake Trail. I always start with the South Cove Trail, which brings me to the top of a ridge, and in the process, gets my heart pumping and my brow sweating small beads.

I eventually descend to the Lake Trail, which is an easy hike, thus more populated.

Recently, I was walking the Lake Trail and passed two young teens who were reciting the Rosary, repeating the Hail Mary, and fingering the glass beads to keep count, I suppose. They seemed fourteen and wholesome, like girls who might aspire to become nuns one day. The oddness of the moment made me consider the religious nature of my regular Radnor walk.

There are certain landmarks on my trail that I liken to the steps through the liturgy, places that always call to mind those whom I love, and my hope that God cares to draw them into a circle of peace. One of these places is a hairpin turn in the trail, overlooking the lake as I descend from the ridge. This is my Kyrie Place, the bend in the road that turns my heart to my Dearest Companion and reminds me of the good graces that brought me to her table. My prayer is silent and steady, until the earth flattens for a moment, and then drops to the road below.

I inhale "Lord Jesus Christ, Son of God" and exhale "Have mercy on me, a sinner."

Minutes later, on the Lake Trail, I take a slight detour to the right, where in spring the purple wildflowers are draped like royal robes across a shaded meadow. There, I find a bench with a name on it, and the dates of the short life that the name belonged to. Often, there are two or three crosses fashioned from twigs placed on the bench, next to the name. Sometimes a small wreath of wildflowers withers next to the twigs. I gather two small sticks and make a cross on a log that lies just beyond the bench.

My little twig cross is meant to announce "Christ has died; Christ is risen; Christ will come again" to anyone looking for a little cross sitting on a decaying log. I gingerly make my way back to the main trail, praying for my children and hers, and anyone else who comes to mind. I ponder my journey, sometimes retracing my steps with remorse, sometimes planning my next step, and hoping that little broken crosses avail much.

Often on the ridge, the least-traveled part of my regimen, my inner dialogue is loud enough to make me wonder if my lips are actually moving, like those of the little Catholic girls who were praying to Mary. Nearly like a dream, where the people you recognize might not look like themselves, my dialogue isn't articulate or poetic, but perhaps more like the call of a wild goose or a lone owl, symbols of Spirit winging through my mind like glossolalia, haphazardly acknowledging broken promises and lost relationships, unresolved conflicts and unsolved mysteries, the sad scars of what is and of what never will be; love, peace, joy, life and death, and the certainty of resurrection. They are both a feather on the wind and the wafer on my tongue.

Recently, I was having a conversation with my friend Dave Perkins about Radnor Lake. Dave is a bona fide rock 'n' roll guitarist, one of Nashville's musical treasures, yet he's also a bona fide doctor, teaching and studying religion and culture at Vanderbilt University. As if that's not enough, he is also a cancer survivor. Dave is my kind of saint, a man who can rip your jugular vein with a slashing blues riff, or talk about the peaty taste of his favorite single malt, and eventually get around to discussions of God and philosophy. Together, we have shared stages, bottles, and ideas for many years.

Like me, Dave grew up in a pointedly religious home, and has probably never been able to shake Jesus, but has certainly shaken many of the notions that Fundamentalism and Evangelicalism had foisted upon him in his formative years. His inability to shake Jesus comes across in his music, and in his living, and in the very essence of conversation with him. While he doesn't wear it on his sleeve, sooner or later, the Word appears, as if carried on the unheard wings of an owl in the darkness.

We talked about Radnor on this recent occasion, and I told him of the liturgical path that unrolls before me every time I begin my ascent of the South Cove Trail. I spoke of the Catholic girls reciting their Hail Marys, and of the crosses left anonymously on a memorial bench, of my Kyrie and my dreamlike prayers, randomly uttered, much like the pebbles rolling off my soles, or the beads of sweat serpentinely running down my brow.

Dave says it's the same for him, coming to Radnor to commune with God. I like how he puts it, "It's all over the place, man. A lot of people go there to get their work done." I think he's right about that, although the thought never occurred to me until I passed the future nuns, passionlessly (so it seemed) reciting their prayers in an eerie monotone. The energy level must be something with all these pilgrims stirring the same mystical cauldron with petitions, prayers and praise, brokenness, fullness, joy, sorrow, emptiness, hoping, hopeless, despairing, longing, exulting, and expectant. How divinely human.

And what of that owl at the edge of the forest, at our journey's end? A good omen? A rare sight? Perhaps she's a faithful watcher of souls, gathering up a thousand prayers from the forest floor, and bringing them to the arms of Mercy at the day's end.

[handwritten margin note: So acceptable to the Word if so unlike Jesus?!.]

6

Ashes

Air blasts from huge pipes and fills Christ Cathedral with large, round, primeval tones, like redwoods reaching toward heaven. The organist is far removed from sight, high on his perch in the balcony with choristers chanting hymns ancient and modern, performing unseen for an unseen God while the congregation below feebly sings along.

It was Ash Wednesday, the beginning of Lent. Ducking into the cathedral a few minutes late, we had missed most of the Scripture readings, catching a sentence or two of the Gospel reading as we took off our coats.

The fact that neither my Southern Born Woman nor I recognized the person preaching made me wonder how long it had been since I'd been in church. The service program read "homily," a reminder to the preacher to keep it short. In an age in which boundaries are few and anything goes, "homily" is a word that pleases me. As it turned out, the speaker ignored the written guarantee and delivered a sermon, which to my chagrin was a reminder that Lent is not necessarily a season of getting what one wishes for.

Lent is a counterbalance to the calendar, forty days in which to remind oneself that we are but mortals in the hands of an Almighty Immortal. I've rarely done Lent like a pro; I'm a day into this season of fasting, and I'm still not sure what to give up. Chocolate? Facebook? Red meat? One year, I suggested to my friend Bryan Owings that I was thinking of giving up snide remarks. He reacted strongly, chortling, "Don't do it!" perhaps worried that I would shock my own system by avoiding what comes naturally.

Growing up with a Baptist preacher for a dad and a Lutheran organist for a mom, I had a slightly more ecumenical experience than your average Baptist or Lutheran, but Lent was certainly not a part of our vocabulary. Given the restrictions that many Baptists live by — no drinking, no smoking, no card playing, no movies, no dancing — I guess there was no need for a Lenten observation. After all, what was left to give up?

Sitting in Miss Putnam's fourth-grade classroom at West Barrington Elementary School, Ash Wednesday always surprised me. There had been no Fat Tuesday Pancake Supper at Barrington Baptist the night before, no warning at all that half of my schoolmates would walk into our creaky old building looking like zombies, the cross of soot looking like an indentation in their foreheads.

By lunchtime, my Catholic classmates' heads no longer had a visible cross, but rather a dark cloud just above the eyes, giving them an ashen, grave appearance. I was pretty sure Catholics went to Hell, but to see them looking so ready for the casket gave wheels to my imagination, and I sadly realized that many of my friends would be in that number below.

Rhode Island being a predominantly Catholic state, Fridays were fish days in public school cafeterias, whether it was Lent or not. In those days, school was started with the Pledge of Allegiance and the Lord's Prayer. I remember intoning the Lord's Prayer for many of my school days, and all these years later, it's difficult to imagine prayer in school as something unquestioned and taken for granted.

By the way, I'm not one of those people who wants prayer back in school. I think a person of substantial faith knows that anything done by rote usually amounts to nothing or, at best, lip service.

My Catholic pals could rattle off ten Our Fathers faster than I could say it once, and of course, the Hail Mary seemed creepy to me; the idea of praying to Jesus' mom. Nowadays, it makes sense to me to appeal to a person's mother if you don't feel like you can get his attention. But in grade school, all things Catholic seemed taboo and dangerous to me.

To be fair, all things Protestant were even more frightful to my Catholic friends. Once, Johnny, a boy who lived on my street, took a bike ride with me, and we stopped in at Barrington Baptist to say hello to my dad. I went into the building, but Johnny waited outside, superstitious that entering a Protestant church might damage his soul in a way that would play itself out in years to come. Wherever he is today, I hope his superstition paid off.

When I was in the sixth grade, my friend Dickie Smith's mother died of cancer. Dickie had two brothers and a sister, all adopted, and all hellions. Dickie smoked and cussed and stole money from his dad and *Playboy* magazines from the newsstand in seedy Riverside, across the tracks. Maybe it's Dickie who influenced my boyhood ideas about Catholicism.

My parents and siblings were on a church trip, and too young to get to go along, I stayed behind with a church family, the Sharps. So, on a Tuesday morning in 1964, Mrs. Sharp and I entered St. Luke's Roman Catholic Church for Mrs. Smith's funeral.

Gaudy and provincial, the interior of St. Luke's was cluttered with gilded saints, something Liberace might have dreamed up. The smoky perfume of holy incense wafted between the pews, strange and unpleasant in its pungent chalkiness. The celebrant's voice rose with melodic uncertainty, uncomfortably singing in a foreign tongue.

The Latin service was unsettling and morose to my young ears, and, worse yet, something disturbing caught my eyes and wouldn't let go. A crucified Jesus hung high in the center of the church, with the most pathetic look of self-pity one can imagine, crimson paint dripping gaudily from a crown of thorns. This crucifix was not quite life-size, giving Jesus the appearance of being perhaps four or five feet tall, and eliciting no pity from me.

This was quite an inauspicious beginning for a future ecumenical. I'm sure I'd been to other masses before, probably a Lutheran or Catholic wedding, but this is the one that I remember, perhaps because it was such a somber affair.

In my life, I have been at some funerals that were joyous festivities, full of certainty in the afterlife, the weight of loss counterbalanced by the joy of celebrating a life well lived. My father's funeral was certainly such an occasion, a common cup overflowing with sweet wine and salty tears. But Dad was in his eighties; Mrs. Smith was probably not even forty.

There were no smiles exchanged at Dickie's mother's requiem mass, no anecdote-filled eulogies eliciting chuckles and nods, and the scent of wonder and hope did not quietly steal among the congregants, kindling a sense of hope and comfort. Rather, the gray perfume of an apparently indifferent and unappeasable God stifled any notion that Mrs. Smith was now resting in merciful hands.

As a child, I didn't know that the requiem mass for Fran Smith was a vehicle in which to pray for her soul's salvation from God's terrible and swift judgment. For one thing, it was in Latin.

> *Forgive, O Lord,*
> *the souls of all the faithful departed*
> *from all the chains of their sins*
> *and may they deserve*
> *to avoid the judgment of revenge by your fostering grace,*
> *and enjoy the everlasting blessedness of light.*

Watching Dickie and his siblings and father file out behind Mrs. Smith's casket made me uneasy and sad for them all. As I watched them, I worried about my mother and dad. Quite suddenly, the possibility of walking behind their caskets with a church full of mourners seemed viable. It was odd watching Dickie, all dressed up, uncomfortable in a starched white shirt, his maroon tie clashing with his wild red hair.

The casket rolled by Mrs. Sharp and me, and as I imagined Mrs. Smith's little body trapped within, I assumed that her soul was now in Hell, unless, as Dickie had told me, the prayers his family had paid their priest to say might bring her weary soul into Purgatory.

This first Catholic experience was simultaneously my first encounter with human death and grief, something worse than the loss of Frosty, my mother's canary, who was replaced by subsequent canaries, all named Frosty, as if he was never really flying off to that great birdcage in the sky, instead continuing to drop dead, eliciting a few of Mom's sentimental tears, then lying stiffly in a shoebox buried by our rusting backyard swing set, until returning to his perch as if he'd never left. If I hadn't been closely watching, Frosty would have made a solid case for reincarnation.

Lent brings me back to reality. To dust we return.

At Episcopalian funerals, I am always touched by the opening words the priest says, following the casket into the church:

"I am the resurrection and the life, saith the Lord; he that believeth in me, though he were dead, yet shall he live: and whosoever liveth and believeth in me shall never die."

It doesn't matter who is lying in that rolling box; my eyes will well up, sad for the mourners, sad for the mourned, yet hopeful enough to be grateful.

I think about my own funeral service occasionally. I have some sort of funeral plan tucked away in a bureau drawer, in the hopes that there will be enough twang and shuffle to send me out like it's Mardi Gras.

Whenever I attend a memorial service or funeral (which seems to be becoming more frequent), I revise the plan. I hope everyone who'll need to hear anything from me will have already heard it. I should go up to my bedroom right now and tear up my plans, and trust my children and my Dearest Companion to make my funeral be whatever it needs to be for them.

Mark Twain tapped into a real human emotion in *The Adventures of Tom Sawyer*, when Huck and Tom found themselves hidden in the balcony at their own funeral service, looking down at who cried the hardest and who missed them the most.

When I'm gone to where I'm going, it's unlikely that I'll even want to attend my own service. But if I do show up, it will be with a new mind, a new heart, and no wear and tear on my old soul. On some rafter, I'll finally be enlightened enough to show up at church without judging, unbothered by the out-of-tune pipe organ, unaffected about who's not mourning, who didn't show, who sang off-key, whose homily turned into a sermon, or who didn't carry out my final wishes. Maybe I'll tear up that piece of paper now, and let everyone off the hook.

No thought of being with Christ! Poor m an.

7

Happy Feet

As teenage boys, my brother David and I had a Yuletide strat-
egy. Our shoulders shrugged with the knowledge that many of our
presents would be mundane—socks, a tie, a tie clip, a devotional
book from Mom, and Old Spice from Dad: The usual stuff. Thus, every Advent, we whispered what we each wanted from his brother. It
would always be a rock 'n' roll recording, the one thing our parents
were not going to spend money on.

Come Christmas, tearing into the wrapped vinyl record, I would
feign surprise, exclaiming, "This is just what I wanted," as if he didn't
know.

Our tradition was to open our gifts on Christmas Eve, as my
mother's Swedish family did. Santa never squeezed his jolly behind
and beer gut down our chimney; Mom guarded our Christmas fiercely
from commercialism by keeping our fireplace stoked and burning, lest
Santa believe he was welcome at 22 Salisbury Road.

Occasionally, Dad would sign a gift tag "From Santa," but that was
all the fantasy we were allowed on this holy night. He didn't seem to
have a problem with the fantasy and the reality coming to terms with
each other, but our mother's scruples ruled the holiday. I didn't care if
Santa wasn't real, but it would have been fun to pretend that someone
beyond ourselves knew our secret wishes, and I never understood the

harm of writing a letter addressed to the North Pole, which would have wound up in a drawer in the east bedroom instead. She may have been guarding her children from the World, but I'm more inclined to believe that she was protecting the Infant Jesus.

Such was the religious fervor my mother approached Christmas with.

Nonetheless, the ghosts of Christmas Past continue to visit me with beautiful memories of joyous times with my parents and siblings. The scenes are vivid and indelible, backlit by warm candlelight.

My mother's liturgical background artfully enhanced the spirit of worship at the Baptist church Dad pastored. And there was no greater expression of this art than in our Christmas Eve service, behind which she was a driving force.

In anticipation of Christmas, our church celebrated Advent, foreign to most Baptists, something that those lost Catholics do. This was my mother's influence; she understood that Christmas was best celebrated as a climactic moment that comes but once a year. So, leading up to Christmas, we sang "Oh come, oh come, Emmanuel" but waited until Christmas Eve to sing "Joy to the World, The Lord Is Come." I'm sure many folks thought, "What's the difference?" but all these years later, my Southern Born Woman and I quite agree that Christmas can only be Christmas for a few beautiful moments.

Between all the shopping, baking, preparing for guests, getting the house decorated (which my mother did exceedingly well), the focus for my parents truly was the Christmas Eve service. There were choir rehearsals, a sermon for Dad to write, a sanctuary to decorate, and music to be chosen. When I became an adult, one of my great joys was my father's annual request that I write a song for the service. He was unwittingly preparing me for my career in songwriting.

One year, the Muse gave me a new understanding of the Incarnation:

As if the sculptor could become the sculpture
As if the writer could become the book
As if the painter could become the painting
the Creator has become part of what He's created!
(from Some Kind of Love ©1981)

As a child, I just wanted to get the service over with, and get home and open presents, but as I matured, the Incarnation became central to everything I believed, and the Christmas Eve service at Barrington Baptist became a warm comforter that I wrapped around my faith on the coziest night of the year.

Amazingly enough, with all the preparation for the service, my mother would have our traditional Swedish meal prepared, and we would enjoy this before heading to the church. Our meal consisted of Swedish meatballs, korv (potato sausage), and lingonberries, and to this day, I carry on that tradition, even to the point of buying sausage casings and making my own korv. For one day of the year, my house smells like the cafeteria at IKEA.

With little time to appreciate the wonderful meal we'd just enjoyed, we would drive through the snow, up Salisbury Road, north on Washington, East on County, and so on, until we got to the church, a mile away from home.

The sanctuary was nearly pitch black when the service started, no light apart from the smallest glow from an illuminated manger scene. The first sound you'd hear was my father's beautiful baritone voice humbly singing "He shall be called wonderful . . ." from Isaiah's prophecy of the Messiah. Then my mother joined in with her tenor — she had a low but lovely voice. Then the choir, and then the congregation, until the room was filled with the words "Everlasting Father, the Prince of Peace." I am moved by this memory even as I write.

My father's sermons were gracious and moving, naturally geared to the "Christmas and Easter" visitor who perhaps didn't believe. (All these years later, I'm somewhat of a "Christmas and Easter" visitor who still believes.) Dad always spoke of Jesus as a lover of the poor, the outcast, the downtrodden, and the loner, reminding Christ's followers that believing the Gospel meant *doing* the Gospel.

The service would eventually come to a beautiful close, and we would be the last to leave, laden with gifts of cookies, fruitcakes, and other such fare from members of the congregation.

And finally, home.

Opening our gifts on Christmas Eve gave us the jump on all our friends, so we quite enjoyed it. As a boy, I wanted what any boy would want—to cut to the chase and open my gifts. Of course, before those gifts were torn into, we had a family prayer time. My mother's fixation on the waiting game of Advent was excruciatingly drawn out until the last possible second.

We would drink a punch made of that Evangelical staple, ginger ale, with vanilla ice cream and eggnog, accompanied by many of the baked goods we'd received from the parishioners, chief of which were the spinster Mabel Matthews's chocolate chip walnut cookies. Finally we'd settle in to opening gifts. My brother or I would be designated the "Santa," truly the only time the old saint's name came up in our household.

One year, I happily unwrapped a copy of *Buddy Miles: Them Changes*, a recording that I love to this day. I went through my tired but effective "How did you know?!" act, and David returned the performance upon opening whatever recording I gave him.

Buddy Miles was a drummer, as was I, and on the cover of this twelve-inch vinyl disk, he sat his obese yet hip visage behind a set of Rogers drums, psychedelically painted in red, white, and blue, like our nation's flag on acid. The music was soulful and bluesy, and Buddy ably kept time while singing in his beautiful black voice, squeezing thick tenor notes through a grinder, the way Santa wanted to squeeze his unwelcome ass through our chimney.

Christmas morning, while the rest of the world's children were discovering what Santa had brought them, we had a leisurely breakfast, opened our stockings, and played with our presents. On this particular morning, I put Buddy Miles on the Zenith stereo and sat in our living room, transfixed and air-drumming.

Mormor, which means "mother's mother" in Swedish, sat across from me glowering, upset that the Lord's birthday would be ridiculed by the Devil's music. In her immigrant accent, she finally hissed, "Vhat do you think Yeesuss thinks of that music?!" as if the Lord's taste in music was identical to hers. I hissed back, "I think He's up in Heaven tapping along!"

I had no love for this woman, who had none for me, and I recoiled from her lame faith that cluelessly celebrated a neutered Christ who gazed incoherently and unemotionally from the pictures of pastures and maelstroms that hung on her apartment walls. She was dismissive of anything secular; her compartmentalization of faith and life made her dreary to be around. I hoped that Jesus wasn't anything like her image of Him, and I imagined Him being bored to tears by her religion.

(I believed in a Jesus I liked) and I credited my father for presenting an earthy Lord to me, a Jesus who wasn't constantly policing my mind, and shoving himself into the middle of every celebration or situation. Jesus might be God, but He's no narcissist.

For all I know, Emmanuel, "God is with us," was indeed tapping along to Buddy Miles's music that Christmas morning in our living room. Isn't that what Christmas is all about? The divine intersection with our profane, fallen lives, Jesus coming down from Heaven and dipping his bare foot in the muddy water of the deluge, swimming with us, pulling us by the scruff of our necks over the crest of a wave, his strong body ferrying weary souls to an eternal shore?

That alone makes my feet tap.

[handwritten margin note: ← EXACTLY— HIS OWN CREATION, NOT CHRIST.]

8

Vunder Bread

I was doing the dishes when the kitchen phone rang. Mom's faltering voice signaled that something was terribly wrong, and in those milliseconds I wondered what tragedy had befallen us.

When she told me that her mother had passed on, I was relieved. I was glad it wasn't Dad, or cancer, or another unmanageable curveball thrown by fate at life's thinly padded catcher's mitt.

I cautiously weighed my words, expressing to my mother that I was sorry for her loss, while in no way sharing the sense of loss. I was not sorry to see my grandmother go.

※

At 102, Mormor had overstayed her welcome. Many years earlier, I had asked Dad how long it would be before she passed. He answered, "Buddy, she's gonna outlive us all."

Fortunately, he was wrong about that.

It was my father who had told me the simple, inane reasons for the grandmonster's hostility toward me. I was eighteen, and we were walking west on Goosewing Beach the day I asked him, "Why does she hate me? What did I ever do to her?" As the sun burned our eyes, he looked straight ahead, squinted, and said that it was really what I hadn't done that had earned her ire. I hadn't been baptized as an infant. I hadn't been born on a lucky day.

Her misunderstandings of me were all wrapped up in superstitions, like a mix of Swedish Lutheranism and the Brothers Grimm. Grim, indeed.

I remember that day at Goosewing Beach, and the afternoon sun drying our skin and swimsuits as we walked. The gentle incline of the ocean floor made me feel like my right leg was longer than my left as we ambled along talking. The gradual curve of the shore gave it a slight arc, thus it was named after a goose wing.

When Dad told me why he thought my grandmother had been hard on me for all these years, I was outraged at her stubborn stupidity. I was also somewhat relieved to know that there was no logical basis for her to be unkind to me; that it was all just crazy stuff with nothing reasonable attached to it.

I appreciated my father's candor in this matter. He must have thought I was old enough to know the truth, and mature enough to know that he was my ally. Realizing that he understood how ridiculous this person was brought me closer to Dad, and made me grateful that he was a witness to the way things really were.

He and my mother were quite traditional and respectful of their elders, thus I never heard them address my grandmother about her ill treatment of their youngest son. Because I never felt defended against her craziness, I'm sure there was some small corner of my heart that believed they must have agreed with her—that is, until that day Dad and I strolled down Goosewing Beach.

Years later, I was told that my mother and Mormor often argued about me. I was glad to know that my mother had defended me, but I think things would have been better had I been a witness to a few of those arguments. It would have done me a world of good to know that my mother had been in my corner.

In the last years of Mormor's century on this planet, she had gone senile and forgotten who I was. When I was in town, I didn't like visiting her, but my mother's insistence upon it was formidable, so I would eventually cave in and make the drive over to the East Side, the classy Providence neighborhood where she waited for The End.

The Christmas before Mormor died, Mom and I got into the familiar, exhausting discussion about why I should visit my "paw sweet Grandmutha who asks fuh you all the time." By this time, my mother had expunged Mormor's record of abuse and just wanted me to remember her mother as the typically wonderful grandmother that most kids have. I couldn't do that. I wanted to forgive the woman, but I wasn't about to rewrite my own history.

To present an example of how my mother tried for years to present her mother as the quintessential grandmother, I will cite the "Mormor's Bread Cover-Up." My grandmother made an amazing loaf of oatmeal bread; I know of no other bread this wonderful. What I didn't realize, until I was grown, was that "Mormor's Bread" was a recipe *my* mother had discovered on a box of Quaker Oats. It was *my* mother who, hoping to give us a reason to appreciate *her* mother, taught Mormor to bake oatmeal bread, and bequeathed it the title "Mormor's Bread." Thus, the only thing I ever liked about my grandmother was concocted by my revisionist mother.

My mother often has both hands in the bowl of our lives, kneading, manipulating, and fixing. What can I say; she loves to bake. It's hard to be a good parent and not want to fix things.

Anyway, appeasing the powers that be, I headed to the East Side, over the Washington Bridge, skidding through snow down the exit ramp, and negotiating a right turn onto Gano Street. I drove past Revolutionary War–era homes, past the Dunkin' Donuts, past the Portuguese Club, and eventually parked in front of the nursing home. I sauntered through the automatic doors, scrutinized by several old-timers in the lobby, who perhaps wondered if I had come to visit them. The smell of urine and old age was everywhere.

How strongly this man reviles/hates his g'mother! Spiritual, not fleshly.

Mormor seemed to know who I was, and was happy to see me. She repeated her questions every two minutes, and I would repeat the answers, realizing that she had some memory of who I was, but lacked the ability to retain new information.

When she asked me what I did for a living, I told her I was a musician, to which she responded, "Oh, what kind of music do you play?" Wanting to see if she had any of her moxie intact, I said, "Jazz," believing her mind was too far gone to relate to the term "rock 'n' roll."

She frowned and said, "I thought you played heavenly music," and I said, "Well, it is heavenly." She quickly said, "How do you know? Have you been there?" amazing me with her wit, on one hand, and reminding me of days long gone on the other. I told her I assumed she'd find out sooner than I would, and she said in a surprisingly matter-of-fact way, "I suppose you're right."

She kept forgetting who I was, and it became difficult for me to remind her that it was Philip, expecting her to express displeasure at the mention of my name. "And whose son are you?"

"Anna-Lisa's, your daughter's son."

"You are?"

"Yep, that's me."

The litany of ask, answer, repeat continued for the entire visit. I just wanted to get to the benediction as soon as possible.

When I got up to leave, she reached out her hand and clutched my wrist, protesting, "Don't leave me!" It was the first time I'd ever heard this voice express any desire for my company.

I pulled the clamped fingers apart and escaped, troubled by her kindness to me, a stranger. When the elevator door closed, I paused in a brief, tearful moment, a moment rife with irony and bitterness. Now that she had no memory of me, my grandmother had been more or less kind to me, wanting me to stay. She was fully capable of kindness to this strange man whom she didn't know, and I experienced a sadness and jealousy of sorts, having experienced my grandmother the way any stranger might have. Her withholding of decency and love for all those decades suddenly seemed more acutely mean.

—⁂—

Thus, upon hearing the words "Your grandmother has passed away," I felt no sorrow.

After the initial formalities had been exchanged, my mother told me she wanted me to be a pallbearer, to which I had no easy way of responding. I didn't argue, but wondered how I could gracefully escape this task. Carrying that casket would implicate me as one of the bereaved. It felt dishonest to me, like pawning something off as Mormor's Bread.

Mom and I hung up, and I called my brother. Neither he nor I was particularly sad about the recent departure of our maternal grandmother. I made comments that made him laugh nervously, as if a lightning bolt might strike me, and then carom through the phone lines and dispense with him as well. The gist of my remarks was "Thank God she's gone."

Eventually, I told him of my uneasiness about being a pallbearer for a woman whom I was well reputed to have little patience or love for. David said he'd take care of it, and we said good-bye.

A while later, my mother called back, her voice quivering with tears, yet demanding an answer for my decision to bow out of the pallbearer role. I explained that I was truly sorry she'd lost her mother, truly. But likewise, I said that I wasn't sorry for myself because I hadn't lost someone who was dear to me, rather, "With all due respect, Mom, she was never nice to me." I explained to her that in asking me to pretend I had any regard for Mormor, she was asking me to deny the many years of mean-spiritedness I had endured. I felt as if I was being lured into a trap with grave consequences (pun intended).

My mother's ability to overdramatize a situation produced a memo-

rable line, framed in her New England accent: "IF YOU COULD SEE
HUH PAW, LITTLE DEAD BODY!" That didn't help her cause, and
I stuck firmly to my guns. Disgusted with my lack of flexibility, she
hung up.

A while later, Dad called. Please remember that my father was
the least manipulative person I've ever met. Dad truly had no self-
promoting agenda, but in this case, his words shocked me and betrayed a sense of desperation that I'd never seen in him before or since
this moment.

"Buddy, if you won't do it for Mom, will you do it for Jesus?"
Ouch.

I was stunned. I quickly gathered my wits about me and said,
"Dad, I'm not doing this for Mom, and I'm not doing it for Jesus, but
I will do it for you because if I don't, you will hear about it until the
day you drop."

So, on a cold December day in Cranston, Rhode Island, under unspoken protest, I joined the grieving heirs of a woman who gave me no
reason to mourn her passing. I sat, emotionless, through the prayers
and eulogies, puzzled by my sister's tribute to the woman who had
taught her to embroider, and saddened only by the knowledge that
quite a different kind of investment had been made in my sister's life
than in mine. I listened to the Swedish hymns of her Lutheran faith,
but didn't partake. It was difficult to imagine that she and I wor-
shipped the same God, and I wasn't about to pretend that she was my
sister in Christ.

After the service, we brought her "paw little dead body" to the
cemetery and lowered it slowly into the barely thawed ground. I felt
a genuine sense of relief as the casket sank, yet was also aware that
something like her ghost would probably be around for years to come.

Back at Bethany Lutheran Church, the cousins, aunts, uncles, and
an ex-aunt gathered around several tables in the basement. We drank
coffee and ate little sandwiches, cut into small triangles of Wonder

Bread with tuna, chicken, or ham salad, only detectable by their slightly varying hues of beige or pink. Let's not forget the large plastic bowl overflowing with Hawaiian Punch. It was as if the reception was being catered by a few old Swedes from Garrison Keillor's Lake Wobegon.

One thing I don't miss about the Evangelical stream of Christianity is the clumsy use or downright absence of alcohol. Bring on the wine for Communion, champagne for weddings, and whisky for funerals. I like to think that Jesus did no less.

The triangular sandwiches were piled high on two platters under a ceiling that hung low, fluorescently lit with a nauseating glow. Kind words awkwardly expressed obligatory remembrances that only a few believed, while the truly bereaved smiled sadly and choked back genuine tears. I felt sorrow for my mother, a good woman trying to do right by her mother, but there was nothing to say. I just wanted to leave.

My brother's son David Ward, about five years old, came over and took my hand, and proceeded to lead me to an old grand piano in the corner. "Uncle Phil, play the blues."

I sat, and started playing a shuffle in the key of C. My left hand played a walking bass melody, while David Ward began repeating a bluesy riff I had taught him on our last visit. Gradually, family members encircled us, until the entire party of relatives completely surrounded us. One by one, my cousins and siblings requested songs. I obliged, playing into the late afternoon, bidding farewell to a woman who hated the music that serendipitously closed down her funeral party.

Later, I was entertained by two ideas. On one hand, I had just danced on my grandmother's grave by playing my music, not hers, at her funeral. I was warmed by the idea of having had the last word.

That's me at my worst.

But there is another side to me, a side haunted by goodness, perme-

ated by what I believe to be true about Christ, the resonant idea that
his gospel is one of reconciliation, mercy, and peace. The better angels
of my nature beckoned me to listen to what beauty might have been
present when my nephew asked me to "play the blues."

I pondered this woman of odd faith, superstition, sternness, and
joylessness. I reckoned that she really did believe in Jesus, although
not in any kind of generous way. Yet, what if she had been enfolded
into the arms of a waiting Parent on high? What if she had beheld the
Almighty's light, as I hope to behold it one fine day? Furthermore,
if she was in that "cloud of witnesses," wasn't it fair to assume that a
bonus therein was for her to witness her own funeral?

Assuming her spirit was with us in some form or fashion, and assuming the cloud on which she was eternally perched (and harping,
no doubt) was in close proximity to the church she'd worshiped at for
decades, it wasn't hard to imagine her being present in the basement
of Bethany Lutheran when I started playing requests. Maybe the inter-
mittent buzzing in the fluorescent light fixture was the protestations
of her ghost.

In my more generous moments, I like to think that she was looking
down with her newly enlightened mind, and that she got it, got *me*.
And if that truly was so, then, she might have finally been able to
celebrate the lives of people she didn't understand. Perhaps, as an enlightened soul, she understood all her heirs in a way that we couldn't
even comprehend until our day of going Home.

I've always been grateful to my nephew for his innocent request to
jam with his uncle. It didn't change my relationship to Mormor; I
couldn't erase her presence in my life as a crucible of sorts. However, our
little jam session did afford me the opportunity to ponder her as an eternally forgiven soul, whose road brought her to the literal end of herself,
and to a resurrected goodness and unconditional lovingkindness.

That's where I want to go. Until then, if you want, I'll play the
blues.

How arrogant! Like he's already 'enlightened'!!

Mormor's Bread

Pour 2 cups boiling water over 1 cup rolled oats and let stand for one hour.

Dissolve 2 tablespoons yeast in 1/2 cup warm water.

Add the oats, 5 cups of flour, 1 tablespoon shortening, 1/2 cup molasses, 1 teaspoon salt. Knead. (Add or reduce flour amount according to dough consistency.)

Let rise one hour.

Punch down and shape into loaf.

Place into two greased pans.

Let rise 1 hour.

Bake at 375° for 40–45 minutes.

9

Crescent Park

What is it about the human condition that makes us crane our necks and try to get an eyeful of the seedy little town next to Paradise?

If you walk about a half mile north from Salisbury Road, the street I grew up on in idyllic Barrington, Rhode Island, everything changes. In Riverside, the kids are meaner, the potholes are deeper, the homes are smaller, and the next time you cross the border, you'd better bring your big brother.

There isn't much allure left to Riverside now, except for the "package store," as Rhode Islanders call liquor stores, and the Carousel.

Barrington citizens live in a dry community, and thus drive across the town line to buy liquor from package stores in neighboring towns that have poor zoning along with plenty of booze.

Riverside is a village that sits on the northeast banks of Narragansett Bay, and had moderate fame in the early 1900s as the home of Crescent Park, New England's Coney Island. The only remnant of this amusement park is the beautiful Looff Carousel, built in the late 1800s by a German woodcarver, Charles I. D. Looff.

The Pharisees of my childhood were sure that the Devil's music was rock 'n' roll, but I always pictured Old Scratch sitting behind an out-of-tune calliope, whose pipes sent mutated polkas and eerie invitations to permeate the slingshot dreams of twelve-year-old boys like me.

When I was a boy in the sixth grade, nothing seemed more appealing to me than walking down Promenade Road, across the town line, past the marshes and inlets, to Bullocks Point, which must have been glorious before the Depression. Surrounded by water, the Point was dotted with vacation homes that had been winterized and sold by people who could no longer afford two homes. By the 1960s, the affordable homes were jammed together tightly, so that you could barely see the bay from the little streets that crisscrossed the Point.

Once a community of fishermen and clam diggers, it was Rhode Island's version of a redneck neighborhood, but instead of rusted-out Buicks and DeSotos sitting on cinderblocks, there were large, tubby boats of all kinds in every other yard, dwarfing the homes their skippers lived in. These old boats sat there rotting under canvas tarpaulins, while tempting their owners to keep dreaming about next summer.

I'd walk past the tiniest homes, intrigued by the thought of living in a matchbox. Crossing the railroad tracks, I was conscious of the demarcation and of my alien status as a person from wealthy, uppity Barrington. I was with a neighbor boy whose name was Richard; we weren't close friends, but he was the only person who dared go with me.

Richard and his mother were English, and his proper way of speaking seemed odd and sissylike to the boys on Salisbury Road. Richard's father had been a soldier in the German army during World War II, so we were quite inquisitive about him. That poor kid was always having to explain that his father wasn't a Nazi, and all these years later, I wish I'd been nicer to him. We taunted him after every episode of *Hogan's Heroes*, assuming his father was like Colonel Klink. I now appreciate this boy's willingness to stand up for his dad, and it saddens me that I was a part of his misery.

I didn't have anyone else who was brave enough to steal away with me into the early June afternoon out of Eden's gate and over the tracks to Crescent Park and its rabble of Philistines. So, I chose Richard, Nazi or not.

Understandably, my parents had no affection for the park. My father would drive us to Rocky Point Amusement Park, across the bay in Warwick, or to Lincoln Park in Massachusetts before he'd bring us to Crescent Park, a mile away from home. I'm not really sure what the difference was, a carny being a carny, but that was the way it was. My folks warned me about perverts and weirdos working the midway and rarely was I allowed to make my way to that forbidden world of dizziness and nausea, so appealing to me as a boy.

The "Comet," a roller coaster, had long ago been retired after someone had been killed in a grotesque accident of urban myth proportions. It stood rotting like the neighborhood boats, and I would gaze at its whitewashed timbers and dream of next summer. Like those crumbling, landlocked cabin cruisers and catboats sitting nearby, the Comet wasn't going anywhere.

Still, the draw was strong.

The harshness of the place made it scary and exhilarating. Tough, muscle-bound greasers stood with cigarettes that seemed to be glued to the lower lip, never falling from the mouth, bouncing gingerly as the smoker talked unceasingly. It was hard to believe I was only a few steps away from Barrington, because in Riverside people spoke with a completely different accent, soft on the letter R ("cah" for car), hard on the letter D (pronounced T à la Davit instead of David), with the strange pairing of a V sound when a word started with the letter R, as in Vronald Vreagan.

Crescent Park was pronounced Cvezent Pahk.

Even at twelve years old, hearing an attractive girl speak with that accent was a deal breaker, not that there were any deals to be made, but I just couldn't bring myself to have a crush on anyone who spoke this way.

Except for one—Sue Pierce.

I thought she was a doll. She was forced to attend my father's church, which is how I knew her. Sue was as cute as they come, and even with that abominable accent, she had a sweet spark, which handily ignited her junior high cigarettes. She was tough and pretty, and probably heading down the wrong road. But when I was twelve years old, Sue Pierce was the sexiest thing I could think of.

I probably assumed that if I hung around at Crescent Park long enough, I'd surely run into Sue, who lived near the park. But I never did, and if I had, what would have happened; what would I have wanted? At twelve years old, I didn't know, but I'm quite sure her presence wouldn't have calmed the madness the thought of her had created in my stomach.

From the Tilt-A-Whirl to the Flying Fish, Richard and I ran, making the most of every minute. I remember riding with him in some sort of swinglike contraption that was suspended high above the ground, going round and round, and feeling conflicted or perhaps convicted that I was not a good friend to this lonely boy, nor did I know how to be. Why I even remember him is strange because I think they moved away after a year or so of living in our neighborhood.

Who could blame them?

I just wanted an accomplice in my adventure. I couldn't find Huck Finn or Tom Sawyer, those sons of the Mississippi, so Richard the son of a German soldier was going to have to suffice. He'd have been of little use to me if the thugs of Riverside had descended upon us. We'd have been no match against the sons of clam diggers, their biceps bulging from raking clams through the Narragansett muck. And God Almighty knows I would have been of little use to Richard either.

Yet, there is something comforting about going into the enemy camp with an ally, no matter how little you feel toward each other. Richard and I said little, if anything, to each other, as if fate had thrown us together in an adventure that would yield no treasure and no fraternal bond.

I don't particularly remember our time in the park as being fun. Perhaps knowing I'd disobeyed my parents' rule not to go to Crescent Park had given me a sense of foreboding. The quick rides stole our dimes quickly, and the time passed more slowly than we'd anticipated. We ate funnel cakes, deep-fried dough covered in powdered sugar, wildly appetizing yet, once eaten, mortally wounding.

Finally, we trudged back to Salisbury Road, penniless, yet unsated, like prodigal sons, hoping our parents wouldn't be waiting at the top of the street.

My mother asked where I'd been all afternoon, and I can't remember the lie, but I suspect I told her that I had been playing in the woods near our home. I am not a great liar in adulthood, not that I don't try, so I imagine that I wasn't a very good liar as a child. Nonetheless, Mom didn't press me further, and that was that.

Or so it seemed.

A few hours after I'd gone to bed, awakened by my good angel, I got up and knocked on my parents' bedroom door. I went in and told them that I had lied about where I'd been, and that I had gone to Crescent Park, and now felt very guilty about having disobeyed them.

These were the moments in which my parents shined. On several occasions, I brought my confessions to them, and they never flinched. Once, I made the confession that I had stolen fifty cents from a neighbor child's room. Another admission was that I had hidden her bicycle in the woods near her house. Of course, I had to face her and her folks and make things right, but my parents' love and forgiveness gave me the grace and courage to stand up and admit my wrongdoing.

Yes, I still rubberneck over the fence to see how crazy our world can get. The part of me that is fixated on God Almighty still clings to the idea of an involved Creator who cranes His almighty neck and peers deep into my seedy soul, and wants to make that His dwelling place. So, once in a while I try to make room for Him, by sweeping out the trash and clutter, but it's a hell of a job.

About ten years after my neighbor and I had our adventure across the tracks, I found myself working a summer job operating the Flying Fish ride at Crescent Park, wondering whatever happened to Richard the soldier's son, and Sue the clam digger's daughter. I hoped that Richard had found good friends, and I hoped that Sue's teeth hadn't completely turned yellow after years of smoking Winstons.

After that summer, I returned to Taylor University in Indiana for the fall term. When I came back to Rhode Island for Christmas, the park had been razed. Old enough to see it for the dump it really was, I felt no sentimentality or loss as I drove past on my way to the package store to buy a six-pack of Narragansett Lager. But I did remember the childhood spell I would fall under when summer winds blew southeast, carrying calliope music over the treetops and gray rooftops, and into my bedroom at 22 Salisbury Road.

10

Horse Sense

Phil Bailey must have been one hell of a guy, because my parents gave their third-born child his name. That's all I know about him; I've got his name. Nothing else. He faded away with the state of Maine in Dad's rearview mirror on my parents' move to New Hampshire, and all that I remember are some vague stories about pranks and outhouses from days long before my time.

I had a babysitter named Pricilla who called me "Flip," much to my chagrin. "Philip!" I would retort to no avail. Pricilla was a character—very funny and witty and sweet, and I'm sure if I saw her all these years later, she would still call me "Flip," but now I'd take it a little better. She married a mortician named Karl, and I've no doubt that she nicknames every cadaver that rolls through their doors.

I'm "Phil" to about 99 percent of those who know me. Those who call me "Philip" are either related or are truly intimate friends, except for one guy named Dan, who calls everyone by their Christian name in a condescending fashion. I don't call him anything.

I have grown into my name, but as a young boy, I was jealous of my brother, David, who was named for my father. To make me feel better about the situation, my father told me that my name was a great name, and that it was fitting for a boy who liked horses as much as I did. Philip, you see, is Greek for "lover of horses."

Indeed, the horse has always been my favorite animal. As a boy, along with pictures of Sherman tanks, pirate ships, guns, and airplanes, I was constantly illustrating my schoolwork with horses. Somewhere in a box of boyhood treasures I have a small plastic white horse, a keepsake from a large set of Revolutionary War soldiers that Dave and I played with. It's scratched up and embedded with dirt from the constant handling of a red-blooded American boy's hands.

Our father grew up on a farm in the Amish country of Pennsylvania and shared a horse named Tony with his brother Gene. I used to think what a marvelous thing it was that my dad grew up riding horses. Sometimes, armed with a bunch of carrots, he'd pull his car up beside a horse in a random pasture and feed it with his bare hand, which seemed brave at the time, but Dad knew horses. He loved all animals, but like me, had a soft spot for Brother Horse.

In 1964, our family took a cross-country trip from Rhode Island to Los Angeles and back. It took five weeks, and it was the greatest trip of my boyhood.

Riding in Dad's brand-new, metallic blue Chevy Bel Air wagon, we saw America's wonders—the Grand Canyon, the Grand Tetons, the Mississippi River, and Disneyland. I have many wonderful memories of our odyssey, but the one that involves a horse is from Utah's Zion National Park.

Camping there for a day or two, my parents sent Dave and me on a horseback-riding adventure—a trail ride up the walls of Zion Canyon. We zig-zagged our way up the side of a sheer cliff on sturdy horses, sure-footed and reliable. At one point, high above our starting point, David's horse reared, spooked by a snake. Dave was all of fourteen, and hung on for dear life. He was shaken, but he lived to tell about it, and it made our shared adventure a much more interesting story. Such are the moments that make big brothers heroic.

Two years later, I was fourteen, and my parents had sent me to Camp Brookwoods in New Hampshire. At the time, going to camp for a month was my reward for getting passing grades in eighth grade. Now, I realize that my parents were the ones being rewarded by the absence of their beloved black sheep. It was a well-deserved break.

Brookwoods was full of upper-class boys in Izod shirts, boys with more money in their savings accounts than my dad made in a year. As with many well-to-do camps, there were stables there, and horseback riding was an available activity. Western style was beneath Brookwoods; we learned the proper "English" method, on saddles with no horns to hold on to.

I was assigned a large palomino, sixteen hands high, named Butternut. He was quiet and easy, and the tallest horse I've ever been on. Every day of that long, hot July, I would amble from some sleepy activity—making lanyards or wallets—and find my way to the stable to see my old friend Butternut.

To say I had a way with horses would be an enormous lie. I believe Butternut had a way with me, patient and bemused, much like Bree in C. S. Lewis's *The Horse and His Boy*. He never threw me, reared, or acted up. Maybe he was too old to care, one hoof on a banana peel and the other in the glue factory, but if a horse can be kind and forgiving of a slow-learning boy, Butternut certainly was. We had a riding instructor, but Butternut was the real teacher.

When I was in college, I took a semester of horseback riding for phys ed. It was fun saddling my horse and galloping through the open fields of Nowhere, Indiana, the wind blowing through my hair—back when I had some. These critters had some life in them, and it was a thrill to feel the horse beneath me, surging forward with a gentle nudge of my heels, and riding like the wind.

It's been a long time since I hoisted myself onto the strong back of a horse. I can't even remember when that might have been. But horses will always catch my eye, perhaps knowing my name, *Lover of Horses*.

It's that affection for Horses that makes one shameful story all the more ironic and sad.

We'd been snowed in for a few days, a rare event in Nashville. On the first day of the snow, my friend Tom Howard passed away, a story I've told elsewhere in this collection of tales. After a day or two, Nashville dug itself out, as it always does. My Southern Born Woman and I decided to drive out to one of the many parks that dot Nashville's borders.

We made our way slowly up and down the single-lane drive, and rounded the bend finding our selves grille to grille with a large pickup truck towing a horse trailer going the wrong way on a one-way road.

I was annoyed. A woman got out of the passenger side, and was hoping to wave me past the truck, but I wasn't going anywhere; I had no idea what lay under the leaves and snow on the side of the road, and didn't feel like scraping the belly of my car on some hidden sharp rock. *Besides*, I thought, *what is with these self-entitled people thinking they can drag their asses and their horse's ass the wrong way up this narrow road?*

I was too annoyed to care about the woman's story of rescuing their horse, and of having to drive the wrong way for whatever reason. Hey, for all I know, it was just a story, right?

Of course, my genteel, properly raised passenger was aghast that my first thought wasn't to help them. I sat, not moving, for what seemed like minutes, because of the inconvenience to me, and then finally, half-arriving at my senses (not fully, mind you), proceeded over the road's shoulder with no damage to my car, but having suffered plenty to my soul.

It was an event that she and I fortunately didn't speak of for quite some time. I didn't wish to remember it; I had enough self-awareness to know I'd been an ass, and just wanted to move on.

Some months passed, and we found ourselves discussing why I would be so inordinately put out with these people and their horse. It was a moment of utter shame for me, bitter and poignant and embarrassing, yet potentially pivotal and life-changing. I was repentant and remorseful.

A week doesn't go by in which I don't think about the horse incident. The impact of my own selfishness on that winter afternoon continues to be real, and continues to reveal truth to me about the human heart, and about the ways nature can speak to the human condition.

Of note is that, in this unfortunate episode, I never laid eyes on Brother or Sister Horse. For all I know, perhaps that trailer carried the progeny of my old friend Butternut, who'd been such a gracious teacher to me as a young boy. Whatever the case, once again, Horse was teaching me a lesson.

As I now think on that noble beast of burden, I wonder about my own burdens, and which of them would weigh enough to make such a beastly man of me on that cold Sunday afternoon. Meditating on Brother Horse, I think of the dignity with which every horse carries itself, even under the greatest of loads. And again, I wonder, what burden do I carry whose size leaves no room for me to walk with dignity?

It's said that a tamed horse, returning to the wild, quickly sheds the habits of domestication. With freedom, the Wild returns to the horse, which remembers its true nature. No longer a beast of burden, Brother Horse runs free and noble, spirited and joyous.

I wonder what happened to the horse in that trailer. Sometimes I fantasize that it was set free in some beautiful meadow, never again to feel the weight of so much as a saddle blanket or the cold steel shock of a bridle's bit. And I pray, *Love, free me of the burdens of selfishness and pride, let me run with dignity and beauty, but keep the bridle close at hand.*

11

The Times They Are A-Changin'

In Tennessee, a late February Sunday morning brings with it a number of certainties.

1. The weather will be uncertain. It might fool Nashvillians into thinking spring has arrived, or it might pelt us with furious and icy raindrops and remind us that we shouldn't really do any hoping until March.
2. The *New York Times* will lie, wrapped in blue plastic, on my Dearest Companion's front walk. If I'm in the neighborhood, I'll carry the *Times* into her house, separate its many sections, and read our favorite columns aloud in a particular order.
3. Most of the South will be in church.
4. I will, in all likelihood, not be.

The *Sunday Times* is *the* newspaper, of course. When I was a newspaper boy in Barrington, Rhode Island, I had one or two customers who wanted the *Sunday Times*, in addition to the heavy *Providence Sunday Journal*. In those days, it was half a buck. The *Sunday Journal* was thirty-five cents. My brother and I each had a paper route, and if we'd gotten along better in those days, we might have realized that we had a monopoly in the neighborhood. Who knows what possibilities that would have led to?

Dave was clearly the better paperboy. He was organized, and competent, with his mind on the work at hand. I doubt that he took more than an hour a day to get his papers delivered.

I, on the other hand, took my time, waylaid by a friend here or there, occasionally even paying a neighbor girl named Carole twenty-five cents to finish the job for me. My mind was on music, drums in particular, and I marched to the cadence of a waking dream, mindless about the papers I delivered.

The paper route was the vehicle by which my parents assumed I would finally learn responsibility and organization.

I might have learned something. I just can't remember what.

Sunday mornings, long before Dad was getting ready for church, Dave and I were out on our bikes, filling chrome baskets with fat newspapers, careful lest we tear them on the woven wire. Once torn, a marred newspaper would be reserved for a nontipping or generally grouchy customer.

My least favorite customer was Mrs. L over on Brook Street, whose side porch was a toxic container of cat stench and cigarette smoke. Sometimes, the odor would be so completely overpowering that I couldn't stand in her house long enough to wait for her to count out the forty-two cents for her Monday-through-Friday subscription; I often let her slide. The stagnancy paid off for Mrs. L, I guess. However, I always saved the most ragged newspaper for her.

Another customer, whose name fortunately escapes me, had a small but dreadfully violent dog, probably named something innocuous—Fluffy or Bubbles. Every time I approached its house the dog would charge me. Once, it bit me, tearing my pant leg and the skin on my thigh. The owner came out and cheerily said, "Oh, he doesn't mean anything." I yelled, "He BIT ME!" to which she said melodiously, "Oh, of course he didn't."

On winter days in Barrington, you could expect snow, and on snowy Sunday mornings, my father would wake with his sons, lower the tailgate of his Ford station wagon, and drive us through the deep and drifting snow. We would ride on the tailgate with stacks of *Sunday Journals*, jumping off and back on, quite literally relaying the news.

Those were good days, which still bond me to my father and my brother. Dad was delivering something of a message to his sons, as we delivered the news.

All those years ago, I never perceived myself as a messenger, carrying the *Sunday Journal* to sleeping customers. Indeed, we are all messengers of one thing or another.

I don't know if such a thing as a newspaper boy still exists. Someone delivers the *Times* to my Dearest Companion, but I suspect it's a grown person who needs the extra income, not a boy saving for a new set of drums.

Newspapers are shrinking in size and in circulation. The smell of newsprint, the scanning for a favorite column, folding the pages in a particular way, the sound of a rustling paper—moments our senses take for granted—they are already from an age past, heaped upon the junk pile of yesterday with the scratching sound of a vinyl record, the static of a transistor radio, and the mechanical sound of a radio dial.

Damn, we are getting old. I wonder if our grandparents came to mourn the absence of clippity clops on cobblestone streets? I wonder if my mother misses the crackling sound of electric streetcars. (I can remember that sound, which I identify with the city Providence, but not enough for it to have made a real footprint on my aural landscape.)

I miss the sound of recording tape running off the spool, flapping wildly, wreaking havoc. I miss the sound of tiny hammers whacking ink onto white paper as typewriter keys are being struck, the imperfect rhythm of a furious mind at work.

Things change.

Yet, some people don't. I think about Mrs. L in her brackish, shuttered house on Brook Street, cigarette butts piled high in receptacles on her closed-in porch. What a metaphor! *The Closed-In Porch*...sounds like a Tennessee Williams title, doesn't it? And the clueless dog owner, unwilling to see the evidence that her pooch had indeed bitten me. It's odd to me that the recluses and the clueless even want a paper, although Mrs. L's cats certainly could have made use of it.

Roll over Beethoven and tell Tchaikovsky the news.

On a recent Fat Tuesday morning, I was startled awake by an incessant knocking on my bedroom wall. It was early, and I was groggy, but I recognized the haphazard rhythm of a woodpecker, insistently head-banging, something that I would, of course, take personally.

I pondered as he pounded. I wondered about God's creature visiting my home, and I decided to embrace this quite natural occurrence with a sense of spiritual openness. No, the woodpecker wasn't prophesying, but I took its knocking as a friendly wake-up call to seize the day, to expect a full measure of effort from myself and to listen to the world around me. And what better timing than for Woody to be knocking away on the day before Lent, that season in which my senses would be heightened, and I might be at my most contemplative and receptive.

Just the fact that I didn't get out my pump-action Daisy air rifle and end the hammering signified that perhaps I was still in flux, still changing, shifting, and embracing another way to look at life.

I sent a haiku about my morning visitor to my Southern Born Woman, who promptly researched the meaning of the species in mythology and folklore. Among those who pay attention to the family of animals, woodpeckers symbolize the need to allow for a change of attitude, and the embracing of opportunity and creativity.

It wouldn't be the first time an animal has taught me something; you may have read other chapters in which I speak of the horse or the owl quietly reminding me that my journey is not over; there is more to learn and more to change.

So, perhaps, I could learn from this tenacious, insistent creature to keep knocking on doors, to continue to pursue dreams and excellence, to strive for those who depend on me, and to stay open-minded.

Good morning, Brother Woodpecker. I'm listening.

12

Sliding

I was in tenth grade at Barrington High School when I fell under the spell of a National guitar. Commonly called a dobro, the body of a National guitar is usually made of brass, and it has a pie-plate-shaped cone in its belly, which acts like a radio speaker, resonating with the strings, and projecting its sound with a beautifully guttural bark, a remembrance of its painful birth in the foundry, as opposed to a quiet origin in a spruce forest like most guitars.

The music I heard was being played on WBRU, Brown University's FM station. BRU, as we called it, played a melting pot of American music, taking the listener from blues to country to psychedelia within twenty minutes. The music that stole my heart was played by a fellow named Taj Mahal, an educated, northern-raised black bluesman who mixed country and blues with a taste of bluegrass. What drew me in was the slippery sound of that National guitar, played with a bottleneck, sliding across the frets, never articulating a perfect note, but hovering around it with uncertainty.

The notes falling out of Taj's mouth dripped with honey and salt, whisky and lemon. His melodic phrases always ended with a sinking note, falling off, dropping low, and heading South. He sang of his baby leaving him, or of his "Big Kneed Gal," a heavy-hipped woman that he couldn't get enough of, although he made it provocatively plain that there was plenty of her to enjoy. He rolled gospel melodies into good-time rhythms that made me think surely God Almighty must love the blues, so much did this music speak to my soul.

It was that National guitar of his that resonated the loudest in my bluesman's heart. Far away from my piano lessons, with their perfectionist demands and every nuance of the music defined by Italian words like "fortissimo" or "pianissimo," Taj played notes between the notes, gray and blue, not black and white, straining toward the finite, but remaining unsure, quite like my simple faith.

I have always believed, since a young age. My father's humble outlook and his genuine love of people was a reflection of his inner life, a life he had dedicated to God. His life is encapsulated by the prophet Micah's words "to act justly and to love mercy and to walk humbly with your God," words that were written in his Bible, a gift from his father. Unlike many in his denomination, he didn't have strict and strident guidelines about what defined a Christian. Christianity wasn't about all the things one shouldn't do; rather it was about embracing a loving and sacrificial Christ who loves all people without question.

In my vocation of music, there seem to be more preachers' kids than in any other line of work. And most of them have tales of treacherous fathers who demanded perfection, proclaimed damnation, and laid down the law on the posteriors of sons and daughters who are now more likely to trust in the bottle than the Bible. They grew up fearing Hell, afraid to fall asleep lest Christ return to find them in a nocturnal moment of blissful shame.

I never feared Hell, and if I thought about such a place or state, I didn't worry about finding myself there. But that's another story.

I have never been able to escape Dad's way of faith, even when I've wanted to abandon Christendom and its crazy, hateful, blind Pharisees. Sometimes it seems to me that many staunch and staid Christians aren't believers at all, but just a collection of fearful schoolmarms and security guards who want to keep God under lock and key. When I want to reject that world, I remember Dad's unwillingness to box God in, or to proclaim "us" versus "them." He wasn't perfect, but he sure tried to love everyone well. That's how I want to live.

Listening to those uncertain notes that the bluesman plays with a bottleneck on his pinky finger, I am inclined to let God Almighty slide as He will, dipping low into His world, and sharing His cup with any who might partake, not worrying about changing or chastising his broken children, but singing in a low guttural hum, forged in the heat of His passion for humans, a God Almighty love song.

He doesn't see death - dealing his pride.

13

Mantle

The sound of the organ at Fenway Park swirled and vibrated far from home plate, gliding like a roller skater up to our cheap seats in the bleachers. Dad brought my brother and me to the Green Monster a few times a year, sitting among the Philistines in our New York Yankee jackets and caps, taunting the Red Sox, who couldn't beat our Yankees.

We watched Mickey Mantle, Whitey Ford, Roger Maris, and the rest of that golden team as if they were gods themselves, dusting Fenway's diamond with her own Red Sox.

My father was as pure a man as I've ever known, not a sissy, but a genuine gentleman. I never once heard him curse, yet he seemed comfortable sitting among the profane rabble in the bleachers at Fenway. As the Narragansett lager collected in stagnant puddles at our feet, we'd shell peanuts and drink Coke.

One Saturday, we drove up to Boston in his turquoise and white '59 Ford station wagon with a few pals. I had on a pair of white deck pants that were popular with the sailing crowd in Rhode Island. I'm sure I felt quite stylish.

Once in the park, my friend Wayne and I explored the stadium, visiting the bullpen where Whitey Ford and Elston Howard were warming up. Eventually, we found ourselves knocking on the roof of the Yankee dugout in hopes that one of their invincible number would come out of the darkness and say hello.

By the time we got back to Dad and our cheap seats, my pants had collected all manner of filth, and were no longer blindingly white. Dad smiled in surprise and said, "Philip, how did you get so filthy?" "Well, Dad," I said innocently, "it's a dirty place." As I had many other times, I had unwittingly given my father a sermon illustration.

I've always thought that his simple farm life had given him a will to sink his strong hands into the rich loam of life, never shrinking away from those who didn't share his beliefs. Rather, he enjoyed them and remembered the names of his mechanic, his barber, and anyone whom he shook hands with. (How ironic that this man with a memory for faces and names would eventually get Alzheimer's disease.)

Both of my siblings named their sons David after that great man, and my sister's son inherited Dad's smile, right down to his handsome teeth. Maybe there is a spiritual kind of DNA that will bequeath Dad's character to my nephew along with the heirloom of his beautiful smile. So far, so good.

People who knew Dad often tell me I look just like him, which pleases me. A while back, I noted to my mother that she is the one person who never remarks at the similarities between Dad's appearance and mine. My postulation is that it might be hard for her to reconcile my Dadlike appearance with my un-Dadlike life, tainted by a failed marriage and a life in the marketplace of rock 'n' roll, far from the hallowed halls of what she calls "full-time Christian service."

Both of Dad's sons have strayed a bit from the cozy living room of Mom's Evangelicalism. I'm told that "Dad would be mighty disappointed" that I don't define myself as Evangelical, but it was his tolerance for change that most assuredly allowed his sons to feel safe enough to stray. Now that "Evangelical" is another way of saying "Fundamentalist," I'm not sure Dad would be able to define himself with the E word, either, given the company he'd have to keep.

[handwritten marginal note, right margin, reading bottom to top:] Rejects Christ → the fundamentals of scripture.

I wasn't as successful as Dad was at living a pure life, but that didn't seem to affect his respect and regard for me. His purity didn't arise from a sense of guilt or fear, but out of a genuine desire to please his God, and to walk humbly before Him.

The idea of being compared to Saint Francis would never have occurred to Dad, but indeed, he lived Francis's credo well: Always preach the gospel, and if you must, use words. Like the beloved saint, Dad loved animals and people, he loved working men and women, yet moved with a confident ease among the rich socialites who found themselves drawn to his quiet presence. The reason for his relaxed stride in the halls of the wealthy was simple: He wasn't impressed by status, wealth, or affluence. Neither did he judge those things.

He was his own man, motivated by his conscience and his principles.

Lest my accolades drip with too much perfection, Dad was human enough to be annoyed by the legalists, bigots, Pharisees, and malcontents of his flock. He didn't often voice his displeasure, partly because he wasn't particularly vociferous and partly because he wasn't prone to gossip. I know he was happy when the spiritually superior would give up trying to change him, and leave for a loftier, "spirit-filled" church.

If he was intolerant of anything, it was pettiness. And Lord, pettiness abounds in the Church.

Dad's upbringing among the Amish and Mennonite communities of his Pennsylvania home had indelibly marked him as a man of peace.

His ancestors had immigrated from Switzerland and Germany in the 1750s. Their name was Madoori, but was altered to Madeira, a popular drink of the day. Given their Anabaptist heritage, it's my guess that they never touched a drop. Nearly three hundred years later, I am often asked by people of Portuguese ancestry if I am a Portuguese and Jewish, as my surname is apparently a Jewish version of the name Medieros.

Trips to my Grandma Madeira's home in Lancaster were always exciting and intriguing. Dad's parents had been wealthy people until the Depression, going from an upper-class stature to a simpler farm life.

In times of plenty and in times of less, my grandmother, Elsie Madeira, was a woman of God. Over her braided, uncut tresses, she wore a sheer bonnet called a "prayer covering," her face unadorned by worldly makeup. Her mother, Anna Lehman, was even more so a "plain person." She wore the equivalent of Amish garments, looking like someone straight out of the 1800s.

I found it fascinating, even as a very young boy, to behold this very strange and wonderful woman who seemed quite ancient to me. In one very old photograph, I am standing at her side showing her a picture of a horse in a coloring book. I am shirtless and shoeless, wearing a pair of shorts, which must have seemed quite immodest to this woman whose outward appearance was all about modesty.

Yet, in the photograph, she looks delighted and interested, and not worried that her great-grandson isn't being raised to be "plain."

A beautiful memory is that of my mother reading the Bible to my great-grandmother, whose eyesight was gone. Mom loved my great-grandmother, who may have been tolerated as old-fashioned and odd among other family members; Mom understood that Anna Lehman and her quilt-making, psalm-singing contemporaries were trying to disconnect from a culture that was at odds with the mystical life they pursued through sewing, cooking, and helping.

Grandma Madeira's earthiness was at once charming and jarring. As youngsters, we were scandalized that she would use the bathroom and leave the door open, while she thought nothing of it. Apart from that odd habit, she was fun-loving and industrious. She was a wise businesswoman who had made a life for herself after my grandfather had passed away in the forties.

She was generous yet frugal, and drove a fabulous split-windshield 1951 Pontiac until 1962 when she bought a very modern Chevrolet Corvair.

It is of note that religion played an extensive role in the households that each of my parents grew up in. As a child, I had great disdain for my maternal grandmother's religion, and a curious awe for my paternal grandmother's faith. Oddly, the trappings of belief were even more pronounced among my father's people than among my mother's. But I believe that these earnest Christians in Lancaster cornered the market on humility, and that is the gift that growing up with these intriguingly simple women gave my father, the most humble man I have ever known.

I've always believed that Dad might have been a different person had he grown up with the wealth that his parents had once known. Instead, he grew up with cows that needed milking, and fields that needed tending. His manly hands and his strong body were built by the hard work of farming, and his keen mind was informed, much like his Lord's mind, by the agrarian work ethic.

He was a strong man, but I never saw him raise his fist or act in a macho manner. In the heat of the Vietnam War, Dad preached sermons that questioned the "Love it or leave it" mentality of many Americans. Though his opinions occasionally went against the grain of his congregation, they found his loving manner to be irresistible.

A trait that I wish I could say was shared by other preachers was that he refused to let anyone know whom he voted for or what party he was a member of, if any. There were no bumper stickers on his car, which, by the way, was usually a nondescript Ford, or a Pontiac, never a Lincoln or a Cadillac.

He owned one pair of dress shoes at a time, and when they were too far gone to be respectable, he wore them when he painted the house, or mowed the grass. He was the original recycler.

Dad never asked the deacons for a raise, and he and Mom tried to live frugally enough to give away as much as possible, a character trait that I both admire and mildly resent, being an heir to a ravaged estate. Enjoying a modest life, he rarely indulged in luxuries, thus yielding common pleasures that much more enjoyable. He lived a truly healthy life.

Before his death, Mickey Mantle remarked, "I'm no role model." A self-acknowledged failure as a father and husband, his sports achievements paled as he looked back at years given to excess. "If I knew I was going to live this long, I'd have taken better care of myself."

Long after Mantle's legs had finally given out, after the Bronx Bomber could no longer swat baseballs over the high walls of Fenway Park, Dad remained a hero to my brother and me, consistently batting close to a thousand in the game of life.

Once in a while, a parishioner would tell me that I was going to be a preacher, just like my dad. I knew this was never to be the case, and certainly hoped they were wrong about my vocation, but I knew I was the recipient of a blessing from the many who made this pronouncement to me. In my soul, whatever remains of that boy still wishes, like all boys, to be like his father.

I chose quite a different path than my father, and never felt quite worthy of his mantle. I couldn't achieve a balance between vulgarity and grace, confrontation and passivity, and it took the severe mercy of divorce to bend my back far enough to let go of the burdens I had strapped onto it.

I have yet to love God in the way my father seemed capable of. My father never once questioned God's involvement in his life, and continually praised God for the smallest of blessings.

On the other hand, I'm trying to pin God down, and remind the Almighty that He needs to live up to the integrity my father imbued Him with. I've spent a few years flailing the waters, trying to keep swimming as the waves rise. Having had a few capsizes in my life, I imagine myself and my image of God waiting it out on some craggy reef in a Mexican standoff. I can't get rid of Him, and He may come in handy once the tide goes down.

It seems like that has been the case forever, but even in the wreck-

[handwritten marginalia: This encapsulates this man's bleak spiritual condition.]

ages of life whatever Dad imparted to me of God-awareness has been a strong Presence.

I don't do God like my father did God. I don't rise at six and spend an hour in prayer. I believe God is in the room, but I guess I'm waiting for the Almighty to begin the conversation.

Dad would sweetly argue that God has done just that.

Ah, the caveat... *I know too much*. Scripture tells me that I'm more blessed to believe without seeing a miracle, a sign, a vision. In that case, I'll take a little less blessing and a little more magic. I'm tired.

I've been left with a burden—the mantle of responsibility to a truth that seemed too easy to trust when Dad was living. Now, my shoulders are aching with the weight of hope, and I'm inclined to empty the burlap sack of everything I know about God except for the instance or two in which a familiar yet inexplicable Presence has overwhelmed me.

Oh, for that to happen often enough to nourish me and seldom enough to keep it beautiful.

As I have aged, my search for a quieter expression of belief reminds me of Dad's quiet trust in the unspoken way of faith. I remember him less for his words, and more for his actions, his humble and friendly demeanor, and his million-dollar smile that betrayed the joy in his heart in a way that few words could aspire to.

My knees may buckle under the weight of his mantle, but my heart will forever be lighter because of Dad.

14

Charlie Baker

Eighth grade, *West Barrington Junior High School, and I can't concentrate. The Turtles' "You Baby" is in my head, and I love the beat that drummer Johnny Barbatos is playing. It's the first week of school, and the weather is intoxicating; I'm looking out the window onto a green meadow.*

But I'd better wake up and start listening, because my English teacher, Charlie Baker, doesn't tolerate a daydreamer. Mr. Baker wants all the attention for himself, and damn it, he will have it. His bulbous eyes stare threateningly and steadily as I hear him say, "Madeira?" the tone lifting so as to present a question, far worse than a scolding, which asks nothing, demands only silence and attention.

I have no idea what Charlie is asking of me. I've gotten off the page for a moment. He moves on to someone else, but I am ashamed and agitated. This won't happen again. Charlie, as we call him behind his back, suffers no fools, and for the first time in my life, I've walked into a situation in which there is no loafing, no floating, no easy way of making the grade.

The announcement that we will be graded on how well we keep notes is shocking. Isn't it bad enough that we have to sit there and learn all this meaningless stuff, and be tested on things we can't imagine using? As if any of us will one day grow up and write a book? The nerve of Charlie Baker to grade us on our notebooks!

I was following in the footsteps of two high achievers, my siblings, Annie and Dave. Being the baby of the family had its advantages in some ways. I escaped many responsibilities that Annie, the oldest child, was laden with, and that, to some degree, Dave, the oldest son, shared. But the other side of that shiny penny was about to get flattened on the railway track of junior high school, and Mr. Baker was my first encounter with a teacher who wasn't about to let anyone escape success.

For at least the first seven years of my life, the First Day of School contained a familiar welcome by each new teacher: "Are you Ann-Elise Madeira's brother?" Or, "Are you David Madeira's brother?" Following my nod, he or she would say, "I'm going to enjoy having you in my class."

Alas, this prediction rarely came true, unless, of course, they had a good sense of humor. In that case, they might have enjoyed the nine-month task of ferrying me across the wide river of whatever grade I was in. I was witty and sharp and essentially turned in my work, but without much dedication to truly learning what was being taught, unless I was interested in the subject.

I had a unique vision, and as far back as third and fourth grade, I wanted to design my own way. This, of course, didn't work well in grade school. Take, for example, the wonderfully old-fashioned Miss Putnam's fourth-grade class, in which we were given the assignment to make Christmas cards, but without any reference to the iconic Santa. (Ironically, there was no moratorium on the figures of Mary, Joseph, and Jesus; how the times have changed.)

Perhaps it was the fact that Santa didn't exist in my family's celebration of Christmas, or perhaps it was the mere suggestion of censorship, but I took the challenge and made a card that pictured a fireplace, with bricks coming loose, and dust falling to the floor, with the caption, "Don't worry, he'll get through."

Being the Funny Guy was my job, both in my family, as the last-born, and in school. Humor served as a great defense, a lively distraction, something to keep mundane things interesting. If I had the entrance, believe me, I would take it, and I must have exasperated any of my teachers who allowed for a split second of anarchy. Somehow, I never made the connection that a quick wit might have to a sound mind, and I learned to see myself as an average achiever, with little interest in producing a body of excellence.

That all changed with Charlie Baker. Charlie wasn't interested in coming down to our level, in being liked, in being relevant. His insistence was far loftier; Charlie demanded his students to rise to *his* level. So emphasized was our need to remember every word he uttered that my notebook included the most banal of facts, having nothing to do with literature.

Again, the Santa connection (and how strange and telling that I remember all things related to the Saint banned from my childhood home). Right before Christmas, Charlie Baker was lecturing, about what I can't recall. He tossed out a remark having to do with the color of Santa Claus's mittens. I dutifully wrote this down. *You never know*, I reasoned.

I'm not sure about the exact literature we covered in Mr. Baker's eighth-grade English class, although a few works come to mind, one being the devastating *Ethan Frome*, a dark and cold novelette of New England. But so steely was Mr. Baker's stare that it was easier to become a scholar than to default to my natural habit of being the Funny Guy and shoulder the iron beam his gaze would encumber a fool with.

Somewhere in that eighth-grade year, I realized something. I liked Mr. Baker. He became my favorite teacher, and remains so to this day. The fact was Mr. Baker respected each and every person in his class enough to demand greatness from them. Born out of that respect, I became excited about pleasing my teacher, and wanted to reward his respect with something I hadn't experienced as a student before—self-respect.

Charlie Baker remains a hero to me. But there's another hero in the story. My mother. Mom was the one who smelled the fear that I brought home in those first few weeks of eighth grade, Mom whose encouragement was needed, and for once, not aggravating.

At the end of the year, we were told that we would be turning our notebooks in for a large part of our final grade. I had taken many notes, but my style was messy and haphazard, perhaps worth a C+. Late on the evening before the notebook was due, my mother and I sat together as she typed the entire notebook out. When Mr. Baker returned it with an A+ and the word "Beautiful!!" it was Mom who deserved the praise. I kept it for many years, one of the few pieces of evidence that there was more going on in my mind than the groovy drumbeat of "You Baby."

On the last week of eighth grade, I sweated through my English final exam, and when I reached the end, the bonus question was, "What color are Santa Claus's mittens?"

After all these years, despite my certainty that they are quite red, I will always give the answer Mr. Baker was looking for: green.

The truths and the lies we carry wormed their way into our core with the aid of people who were influential enough to make them last. We will answer counterintuitively if those influences were strong enough.

So, why does one believe one's beliefs? Some stay to the letter of what a parent raised them to believe, and others go completely contrary to what they were taught.

The gatekeepers of theology are often well educated and aware of the loopholes in the system, yet publicly profess what they perhaps privately doubt. And certainly, doubt is a part of faith. They know damn well that Santa's mittens are red, but what does it matter if they continue to proclaim them green?

Meanwhile, I'm chasing the elusive, greased pig of Truth. God is slippery indeed.

15

Salisbury Road

I've been back to Rhode Island only a few times since my parents moved to Connecticut, once for Dad's funeral, and then a few short visits to the beach with my daughters.

On every visit, I have driven down Nayatt Road, under an archway of elms, past the vistas of Narragansett Bay, and taken the long way so that I see the lighthouse at Nayatt Point. I drink in the view sentimentally, and then head north on Washington Road, a long thoroughfare from which small streets hang like teeth from a pocket comb.

I pass the woods on my left, full of childhood memories, and St. Luke's Catholic Church on the right, full of childhood mystery, and then I take a left on Salisbury Road and pass a few small homes until I reach a green mailbox with the number 22 affixed to it.

I'm always surprised at our once-gracious home's small size. I didn't realize how tiny it was until my parents sold it, and I saw the specs—twelve hundred square feet. It now seems very un-American, the fact that five people could live that comfortably in such a small space. I like seeing the site of many good memories, wonderful meals, and happy times, and I am warmed in those memories.

My favorite room in our house was the living room, where our piano sat, and where we spent most of our family time together.

I picture my father taking his Sunday nap on the living room floor, his head strangely comfortable at rest on his grandmother's low milking stool. His white shirt from Sunday morning's service, unbuttoned at the collar, and his tie loosened, eventually, he'd have to rise, fix his shirt and tie, and go back for the evening service.

I picture Mom sitting in the reupholstered wing chair, reading the *Providence Sunday Journal* and remarking to no one in particular about who was in the obituary pages this week.

She has an amazing memory for dates and times, and I don't think she ever has opened a newspaper without stating the day's date and then announcing something that happened on this date in years past. "February fawteenth—that's the day Leland Jones broke his ahm" or "Mahch twenty-fawth—that's the day in nineteen fifty-faw that we moved from Gonic to Barrington."

Of course, what is missing here is the audio presentation of my mother's voice and her distinctive New England accent. She has always spoken in very emphatic tones with an accent that makes me smile to this day. The absence of the letter R, and the emotion with which she will deliver a sentence is quite entertaining, particularly when she is annoyed or confused.

"Whayah AH my glasses?" she'll nearly sing. "THAT is OOHWICKED!" she'll opine dramatically, giving the letter W extra emphasis. The overwhelming favorite of our family has been when her compassion rises within her about some pathetic character, and she will gush, "The poor thing!" but it's really pronounced "The PawWuh thing!" This is her version of the Southern "Bless her heart," which isn't really a blessing at all.

The passion with which my mother has lived is remarkable, and I need only visit my childhood home to remember many vividly played scenes from its walls.

I picture her inside singing her heart out while playing a hymn on the piano, her canary Frosty singing at the top of his infinitesimal lungs. I honestly believe that her exercise wasn't about hearing her own beautiful, low voice, but truly about the notes and words that she was offering to God Almighty.

I picture her marching out the front door with deliberate steps and a stern face, ready to take on our crabby neighbors, the Siders, who were the meanest folks in the neighborhood. You couldn't breathe the air drifting from their yard into ours without being screamed at for stealing. Sometimes Mom's passion came in handy, and I'm thankful that she occasionally gave them what for.

Yes, I can speak of the constraints of religion and the unwillingness of my mother to ever be wrong, but I have to remember that life was pretty good in my corner of the world. Mom felt the good things as much as she felt anything else. And one of the things I have to remember while weighing the things that have disturbed our relationship is my mother's great passion for life.

She would read A. A. Milne's *Winnie-the-Pooh* to us as if it were Charles Dickens. And she read Dickens's *Tale of Two Cities* with a grave sadness, reflecting on its tragic protagonist, Sydney Carton, and grieving for his sacrificial heroism.

A poor Scrabble hand would always elicit the groaned, painful prayer, "O Lawd, whenuh you gonna give me some good ledduhs?!"

That memory makes me smile, while revealing where some of my crazy ideas of God have come from. He is really involved enough to dole out one's Scrabble tiles? No wonder I get sideways with God when the stuff of life goes rancid. If he can get my mother a ten-point Z or Q, why can't he give me a number-one country hit?

No matter. Her theological effect on my life has had mixed results, but at least we had a good home life.

Dad and Mom were both very affectionate with us, and we couldn't leave the house without hearing the words "Love you."

There are two other rooms that I think of when I drive down Salisbury Road. One is the dining room, the site of family discussions, political and social, religious and emotional; as Annie, Dave, and I grew older, this room became more and more special.

We had many wonderful meals together at our small dining room table. My mother was a good cook, although not notably creative, and great care was put into whatever was placed before us.

We had many a laugh around that table, often at Mom's expense. She was an easy target; her passion made her buttons easy to push. Once, when I thought I had gotten the best of her with a juvenile prank, I left the table laughing so hard I had to expel my food. When I returned to the table, I looked at my plate, and sitting among the creamed onions was Mom's glass eye. She wasn't helpless, after all, and that little victory revealed comic genius I had no idea she was capable of.

Once, we were sitting around the table, expecting Annie's future husband to arrive. We'd never met Jim, and Annie was convinced that her uncivilized brothers would give her beau reason to have second thoughts. As she frantically expressed her worries, Dave and I began chewing more and more loudly, mouths agape, taunting her to believe that indeed we would make the worst impression possible.

Of course, once he arrived, we were on our best behavior. When our visit with Jim was over, a ring was on Annie's finger, and a tear was in my father's eye. Incidentally, forty years on they're still together.

The other room that stands out is our screened-in back porch. We took all our summer meals on that little porch. Whenever we had summer guests, my parents would boil lobsters, clams, and sweet corn, and we would share the bounty of New England. I loved sitting there with melted butter on my fingers, and a pile of empty clamshells on my plate.

After we'd all grown up and left, it was fun to return with our families to that porch, and crowd around the table, and celebrate being Madeiras. We sat on unmatched chairs, a piano bench, and a very old church pew, food piled high between two tables of uneven heights pulled together under a red-and-white-check tablecloth. Our feast was gloriously imperfect.

My only regret is that my children were born too late to remember those days, and too late to have known my father when his mind was sharp, and when the smile on his face was one of loving his family. They never witnessed the Madeira clan in its imperfect glory, as those days preceded their births in 1990 and 1992.

The reunions halted when Dave's marriage came to an end in 1988. Unrehearsed for the intricate dance of divorce, our family seized up, unable to curtsy gracefully before the large presence of our apparent dysfunction. After decades of gathering around a generous feast, we lost our appetite as the gangrene of bitterness set in.

And yet, I still remember the good times. For a while, we lived well in those twelve hundred square feet, blessed by love while it abounded.

I slowly drive past, wondering if the echoes of happy times still softly resonate in those small rooms at 22 Salisbury Road. I look in the rearview mirror, until all I can see of my past is a green mailbox.

16

Ever Enough

She means well. She fears that should she disengage from the problems of those she loves, they will crash and burn on the jagged rocks of The World.

So it has always been with my mother.

This good woman has a stalwart belief in all things Evangelical; it saddens her that I bristle in discomfort at the thought of being lumped in with the group I've fled from. She reminds me again that my dead father "would be mighty disappointed" with my flight away from that particular nest, although I'm not sure she's right.

Dad always seemed contented to know that his children carried the light, although none of our lanterns looked exactly alike.

For my mother, my being a Christian is not enough these days. It's not enough that I believe the Creeds, or that I believe in the Atonement of Christ for my sins; not enough that I embrace a Trinitarian God, and a bodily resurrection, not to mention a miraculous virgin birth.

I have to see things her way.

My mother, to be fair, has been an exemplary woman for my entire life. She stood against racism in our all-white community of Barrington, Rhode Island, she was the first woman to preach a sermon at her Conservative Baptist church, and while she'd never label herself a feminist, it was she who asked the right questions that caused her church to recognize women as leaders in the church. This was the stuff of scandal in 1972, and in some circles, it still is.

She and I don't see eye to eye, but I admire many of her traits and accomplishments. I am acutely aware that we share some gifts and talents, the love of music and words being chief among them. Her great gift to me was the nurturing of these gifts.

My mother's love of Mahalia Jackson's music is probably the raison d'être for my obsession with American roots music. I can still see Mom dancing with her young children in our living room as Mahalia belted out "Didn't It Rain?" while the needle in our old RCA Victor scraped and skipped across the ribbed furrows of an oft-used record.

As a teenage paperboy, I took my Christmas tips and bought a used set of drums. They were cheap, Japanese drums with badges that said "Norma" tacked to their blue sparkle shells. Dad and I drove through the snowy streets of our town to collect them from the smoky den of a local family whose son had tired of his brush with rock 'n' roll.

I carried the bass drum toward the parsonage as Mom came out to greet us. She recalls saying to God Almighty, "Lawd, have you given him this gift only to have him wind up in strip bahs?" I guess a drummer's options were slim at the time.

I've always appreciated that her prayer was a question, especially given the fact that she, more often than not, has answers. I'm thankful that she didn't put her foot down and refuse entrance to my drums; had she seen the coming onslaught of continual throbbing and pounding, she might have barred them from our basement. I'm grateful that she was able to believe that the Giver of talent could also be a Navigator for it.

The drums were my life until I was halfway through college, when the songwriting bug led me to guitar and piano. The drums brought me a little bit of glory, some high school notoriety, and a place in a band that traveled to Scandinavia. But eventually, I realized that to be a drummer is to depend on the fact that a band has to need you, whereas a guitarist or pianist can play solo, without ever looking back.

Mom followed my career enthusiastically as it led from one Christian band to another, and took great pride in my using my talents "for the Lawd." As I matured, however, I realized that singing to the choir was not enough for me. I'd been writing songs for years now, and not all of them fit neatly into the sequestered Christian music world. My faith became a bit more private and personal as I grew, although you might not think so by reading these pages. I was less inclined to immediately jump into a spiritual discussion, and felt less pressure to evangelize than I had felt as a young man. This would be seen, by some, as my drifting from faith, but not by me.

Methodically, as Christian music and I had less and less use for each other, God Almighty (or the Devil, depending on one's viewpoint) opened new doors, and the opportunities to play great music became more and more frequent.

My mother seems conflicted about what I've done with the gift she passed my way. When we speak of career choices, she steers the conversation toward the Day of Judgment, and how God Almighty will have a word with me about the misuse of the gifts He entrusted to me. She bristles when I tell her I've written a song for a group called "The Nitty Gritty Dirt Band," thinking, no doubt, that a band with such a name must play strip bars.

She worries about the cost of my disappointing God. Not that I'll burn in Hell, but that, because I've not limited my lyrical content to singing His praises, my entrance to the gates of Gloryland will include a moment of humility in which our Lord will apparently roll his fiery eyes, sigh, and remind me that I could have done so much more for Him, but, well...sigh, I didn't, but well, there's been a place prepared for me, so I may as well come in. Perhaps, He'll slap my wrist while He's at it.

Ironically, it is my upbringing that gave me my belief in the Atone-

ment, and in the notion that Jesus spilled enough of his own blood
to cover a multitude of sins. In light of that, I've fruitlessly argued
that I envision no 8 mm film clips of my most embarrassing and private moments, which is what the Final Judgment has always sounded
like to me. Eternity will seem aptly named if Mom is right about the
Judgment; it will feel like forever.

These are the conversations that I've taken great pains to learn how
not to have. Sadly, I no longer share my successes with my mother,
and I've learned to withhold the details of my life—not that I'm doing anything unseemly. Simply put, whatever I share will be processed
through the filter of her approval mechanism, and a tired conversation
will ensue.

And to be fair, I think she's happy to just know that I'm working.

The Kyrie and a hymn I've been fortunate enough to have had pub-
lished aren't enough to make her realize that I'm trying to be holistic
about my gifts. With her, it's all or nothing. My playing on the stages
of the world with great artists doesn't mean much to her, but if I were
a penniless hymn writer, she would be ecstatic about my career choice.

I'm not prepared to choose between the secular and the sacred; I
don't see them as separate, and I'm not sure that one can't be mistaken
for the other.

Once, after Mom had gone on and on about my negligent use of my
gifts for the Lawd, I said, "Mom, I won't have this conversation with
you. I love you, but if you keep going, I'll be hanging up."

"Yes, I know, but..."

"Love you, Mom."

Click.

I've gone from being the dutiful son to being the nearly negligent
one. I no longer pick up the phone to call and see how life is in
her assisted-living community. Instead, I respond to her mass emails
with a brief, cheerful detail-free email. I tell her that my daughters
and I are well. I don't tell her how beautiful Maddy's blue hair is or

about Kate's lizard-themed illustration project. And I don't answer her question regarding the devotional book she gave me for Christmas 2008, because the answer is, "No, I'm not reading it."

One day a large envelope showed up in my mailbox. It contained a magazine called *Voice of the Martyrs* with a Post-it note attached to it with an arrow pointing to white man surrounded by African natives (presumably would-be martyrs). The man looked vaguely like me, I suppose. The note said, "Phil, what a surprise to find you here!"

I was pretty sure she was joking, and checked in on her just to make sure she knew that I wasn't, in the words of Tennessee Williams, "a Christian martyr, yes, a Christian martyr!"

My daughters and I visit her once a year in Connecticut for several hours. On one trip, we found an IKEA in New Haven, and loaded up on lingonberries, potatoes, Swedish meatballs, and korv, the sausage that I aspire to make at Christmas. When we got to Hartford, the girls and their grandmother busied themselves with a game of Scrabble while I cooked a Swedish meal for my mother, whose ancestors hailed from Gothenberg.

She was delighted that I cooked for her, and it was a wonderful way to avoid a conversation with her while showing her the respect and kindness that a mother deserves. In a small, charitable act I am able to make her journey on the Long Road Home a bit sweeter.

I never imagined having to use strategies and negotiations in this most fundamental of relationships, and even as I write these words, I hope to balance them with an appreciation for the mother who brought me into the world and the way she has brought great bounty to my life.

The year Mom turned ninety, I was scheduled to join the band with Emmylou Harris at the Newport Folk Festival. Emmy, knowing my mother lived in New England, said, "I want to meet your mother when we play Newport."

My niece Jennifer kindly drove Mom down the serpentine road to

Newport, braving the crowds, and finally getting backstage, where the festival officials had made a place for what was probably the oldest woman in attendance.

Behind my Wayfarer shades, I choked back a tear as Mom tottered toward me, her aging frame carrying a formidable personality. I watched as she and Emmylou greeted each other like old family members, both of them carrying the sort of grace that is irresistible, and both of them women for whom I have great affection.

While Mom was being received by my bandmates on the side of the main stage, Elvis Costello & the Attractions were rocking it. A pleasant breeze flowed up from Narragansett Bay and kept us all comfortable as we waited for our turn to take the stage.

We finally plugged in and started playing "Six White Cadillacs," a rocker we'd been opening Emmy's shows with on that run. I had an acute awareness of my mother's presence in the wings as I went from guitar to accordion to keyboard and so on. We sang an a capella song on Mom's side of the stage as she sat intently listening.

Given the breadth of Emmylou's material, I wondered as we performed if my mother was able to see my work as holy and sacramental. Indeed, when we were finished playing she remarked about Elvis's performance and ours:

"That fellow befaw you was good—he was clevah, but all the songs sounded the same. You played all sawts of music; it was wundaful."

The next day, I received an email the contents of which seemed to have forgotten the light that had shined on the two of us momentarily in Newport. She seemed back to worrying about the course of my life, but I didn't care. I was still basking in the glory while riding our tour bus back to Tennessee. My lungs had salt air billowing in them, as I savored the delight on my mother's face after we'd sung our final encore. It was a morsel, but it was delicious, that taste of approval that I seem to have been yearning for these many years.

At ninety, it's remarkable that she would even consider making her way through the crowd at a music festival, and just as remarkable that her mind might be changed, if only for a summer afternoon in sunny Newport, Rhode Island. For a moment she beheld something holistic and beautiful, something artistic that encapsulates all of life; Mississippi mud and higher ground, the life blood of history and the holy spirit that ties it all together into a God Almighty love song.

She still worries, like mothers do. She counts my losses even as I try to move onward from them, making no bones about the skeletons on my front stoop, never mind whatever's left in my closet, holding to stern beliefs when it comes to her wayward son. And perhaps she waits for God's Almighty boot to kick my ass into righteousness before it's too late.

Upon considering my pending judgment, I wonder, is the Atonement not enough? Is it really possible that the faithful will stroll through Heaven's gate only to have their wrists slapped by God Almighty's holy ruler? Did He really hang up on that cross for the sins of humanity only to find that He wasn't enough for Himself?

I don't buy it.

Meanwhile, I treasure the good memories of my mother, while acknowledging sadly that it's difficult for her to accept the shape my life has acquired. She remembers the good days before she lost her son, who seems to have been co-opted by the World, and perhaps it's only a matter of time before he winds up playing drums in a strip bar.

Boom chick-a boom.

17

Made-Up Names

I'm writing from my hotel room in St. Paul, Minnesota, the second time in as many weeks that I've been in this very nonsouthern town. St. Paul is a picturesque city with a town square that's as beautiful as any other in the Midwest. The St. Paul Hotel, where I'm staying, overlooks the square, and is a stone's throw from Assumption Catholic Church, which I had assumed was St. Paul's Cathedral. The building has the stoic, stubborn look that I imagine the apostle himself had, unimaginative and hard, determined to outlast the harsh winters and winds of apostasy that howl at its thick and unwelcoming doors.

So much for assumptions.

I came to town to play on National Public Radio's *A Prairie Home Companion* with Emmylou Harris. When she introduced me to Garrison Keillor, the show's host, he looked at me with that most owl-like visage and replied in a glorious baritone voice, "Phil Madeira…sounds like a made-up name."

I thought of saying, "Look who's talking—Garrison Keillor," but let it slide.

Years ago, I thought about changing my name. I've always preferred my given name, Philip, but most people are too lazy to pronounce both syllables, so I gave in long ago to being Phil. To complicate matters, Madeira is often misspelled by anyone who knows the "i before e" rule. Consequently, I did go through a phase of trying to find a "made-up name," but nothing suitable was coined, and here I am, Phil Madeira.

The other thing Mr. Keillor said was, "You must be from the Midwest," to which I heartily answered, "No." I am not sure what about me gave him that impression. Perhaps it was the large Hohner accordion hanging from my neck, giving credence to a surmised background in polka music. I think of the Midwest as pedestrian and white-bread, and the accordion often bolsters that image, albeit wrongfully so. But I will leave the accordion to defend itself.

I went to college in the Midwest, specifically to Taylor University, in Upland, Indiana. With the exception of Iowa, I'm not sure that there's any more midwestern place than Upland. It's nondescript, in the middle of bloody nowhere. There is literally nothing to do there, which is exactly why a group of stodgy Methodists built a college there in the 1800s.

In the fall of 1970, my parents drove me from coastal New England, across a winding ribbon of highway that carved through Pennsylvania's hills, gradually settling in Ohio, on a level stretch of land that glibly announces "Welcome to the Midwest." By the time we neared Taylor University, where I was to begin my college career, we were surrounded by flat fields of Indiana corn. We literally turned a corner, and there was my college of choice, rising from an endless sea of maize, a horrible sight for a boy raised on the craggy coast of Rhode Island, where history's ghosts had waged wars, where neighborhoods teemed with Portuguese and Italian immigrants, grilling chorizo sausages with onions, sautéing clams and garlic, and where bluebloods dined on crops of lobster and bluefish harvested from Narragansett Bay.

Indiana had, well... nothing.

As we took a right turn and saw Taylor's shallow buildings rising abruptly from the corn, we said nothing. I think we were all hoping that it was some other college, and that we had taken a wrong turn, but alas, that was not the case.

Had I been a more conscientious student, all would have been different. I would have been accepted, like my siblings before me, into that grand institution of Christian higher education, Wheaton College in Illinois. My parents had gone to Wheaton, along with their classmate and friend Billy Graham. My siblings had gone there. My siblings' spouses had gone there. My siblings' spouses' parents had gone there. There was a time when I believed that all Christians went to Wheaton College, "For Christ and His Kingdom."

It must be a wonderful thing to have such a great college experience that you want your children to attend your alma mater. My parents, particularly my mother, loved their Wheaton experience, and certainly thought it would be the best scenario for the education of each of their children.

I was the only person in my immediate family who did not attend Wheaton. I had little choice, after being rejected by George Graybar, the school's registrar, and a former parishioner of my father's church. You have to be pretty damned undesirable to get rejected by a college whose alumni roster includes your parents and your siblings. I always knew George had it in for me.

When I was a senior in high school, I really didn't have a plan for college. I fatalistically assumed that I would wind up at the University of Rhode Island, although I had no idea what I would study. I applied to Taylor because a family friend, Jack Diamond (not a made-up name) went there and did well enough to transfer to Wheaton. Mind you, Wheaton was where I was expected to go.

One day, an admissions counselor from Taylor called and asked if she could visit with my parents and me, as she was traveling through New England. During the meeting, my mother suggested I read some of my poetry to her. I had written a series of poems about apathy pithily entitled "Who Cares About Apathy?" which at the time seemed like a catchy and poignant idea. These poems were actually quite dreadful, but my senior English teacher encouraged my work with an A+, so it seemed worth it to my mother to present it to the counselor. Mom's enthusiasm for my gifts was apparently contagious, and on the basis of the creativity my paper revealed, I was invited to join the class of 1974 at Taylor University in the fall of 1970.

My student number was 70666. I liked that.

Turning that cornfield's corner and seeing my new home was a real letdown. The architecture sagged with mediocrity, and the buildings were separated by great distances on an uninteresting and very Protestant tract of land. I would discover these distances, during miserable winters, to be impossible to traverse without getting wind-burned and frostbitten.

My parents both wore hopeful smiles, believing in some blessing as yet unseen, and blocking from their minds the fact that had I achieved something more, we would be unloading my luggage in lovely Wheaton, Illinois, where much of my spiritual heritage had been forged, and where my parents had met in the mid-1940s. You know the type of smile I'm talking about; it's actually an exaggerated version of a smile, like a grimace, I suppose, which should be called a "grinace." These smiles appear when one encounters grave disappointments, achingly sad truths, and news of misfortune.

In my parents' minds, and perhaps even in mine, I would have my freshman year in a sort of Purgatory, where the better angels of my nature would ferry me across the mundane waters of required liberal arts basics and land me where I was supposed to be, Wheaton.

Parent orientation centered on a church service, which was as interesting and as moving as the sea of corn in Taylor's backyard. After the bow-tie-clad chaplain said the benediction, we walked to the cafeteria, which was housed under a large, white, dome-shaped building, nicknamed, I would soon discover, "the TU Tit." Indeed, it had the appearance of a reclining woman's pleasantly relaxed breast. One time, some pranksters climbed the giant mammary, placed a fifty-five-gallon drum on top of it, and painted the drum pink along with a large circle around it, giving it a very erect nipple, and thus, a much more realistic appearance. The newly improved TU Tit didn't last long.

While standing in line for my first glorious meal, my mother took pity on a tall, gangly, and awkward boy, and began talking with him. Her compassionate mind was thinking, "Pawuh thing," and she took it upon herself to brighten his day by showing interest in him. The complication of her charity was that my father and I were conscripted into the conversation.

"Wheruh you from?" Mom asked. In a moment that makes me wonder if God isn't mean-spirited after all, Ken replied, "Wheaton, Illinois." "Oh, Dave and I and our two uthuh children all went to Wheaton," Mom announced.

The next thing I knew, Ken, the strange Wheatonite, was inviting himself to join us for lunch.

Great, I thought. *My last meal with my parents, and I have to share it with this weirdo from Wheaton.* After our meal, Ken said, "Hey, wouldn't it be neat if you and I turned out to be roommates." I sure didn't think so.

"Yeah," I said.

A half hour later, Mom was the first to walk into my new room, and I heard her say, "Oh, NO!" and then, recovering, "Er...what a suhprise."

Sure enough, Ken was my roommate after all.

My mother's withdrawn protest came from her very keen sense of reading people, and I think that despite her feelings of compassion for someone she perceived as an outsider, she didn't want her son burdened with the task of rooming with him.

He had already chosen his bunk and his desk, and had hung his artwork all over the room. His chosen medium was flesh. Ken was an amateur taxidermist. His work included a stuffed pigeon and a rabbit's head mounted on a piece of plywood. I later would learn that he was a scavenger, and anything left on the roadside would wind up in our room, despite my vociferous objections.

(Ken would eventually transfer to Wheaton, where perhaps he studied taxidermy. Years later, he surfaced in the Colorado Springs area, where he had built a home from scavenged materials. No lie.)

My parents soon left, and I donned my required freshman beanie and set about the work of embracing my new home. I didn't realize it then, but I had just entered the epicenter of Evangelicalism—the Midwest. If I thought for a moment that my home life had been flavored with the taste of Christendom, the spirituality I was about to experience was of a flavorless, overcooked variety, like English pub food without the glorious architecture and ale.

At first, I fell hard, mesmerized by the thrill of being with a crowd who think like you think. My first experience of the sensation of camaraderie was the childhood discovery of a fellow Yankee fan in Red Sox country back in Rhode Island. Now here I was at TU, with fourteen hundred people who all loved Jesus, and who wanted to change the world for Him. It was an amazing thing, like being in a gigantic youth group.

Truth is, that rebel yell in my heart cannot be stifled for long, and eventually my colors will show. My proclivity to be set apart, to be different, to be Phil Madeira, will always override my desire to belong. My rebel yell sometimes manifests itself in the form of a grand profane moment, in which I am exposed as an odd sort of Christian, and subsequently rejected completely or tolerated generously and sweetly as someone who has yet to truly understand the change that Christ demands of His followers.

I'm a lousy joiner.

Like the housekeeper who doesn't do windows, I don't do religion, although I can make a case for doing windows. The case for religion is weak, and no one has made that clearer than Jesus himself.

Think about it. "The Bible tells me so."

Jesus, a good Jewish boy, has himself baptized in a brook outside the temple grounds, and his cousin, John the Baptist, a complete renegade (naturally, a preacher's kid), does the deed. If that single act isn't a repudiation of organized religion, I don't know what is.

To this day, I don't want to throw out the Baby Jesus, just the bathwater and the toxins we keep trying to bathe His image in.

So, I sought out like-minded rebels, but they were hard to come by.

Although I felt a kinship with the rebellious crowd, I was apprehensive about becoming too enmeshed, because most in that scene were frequent drug users. Refugees from religion, there was a bitterness among this group, most of whom had been steeped in midwestern Evangelicalism to the point of spoiling.

I wasn't yet interested in smoking pot, although I had many evenings breaking the Taylor Pledge by splitting a $1.50 bottle of Boone's Farm Apple Wine, or drinking Drury's, a dreary beer served at Newt's Glass Bar, so chicly named because the bar was constructed of glass bricks. Yep, that's how they do things in Indiana.

Eventually, I gave in to my curiosity about weed, and occasionally smoked in the confines of my off-campus room. I remember going to a chapel service, high as a kite, and trying to remain inconspicuous by wearing welder's glasses.

Someone told me I was having fun.

I hold no affection or sentimentality for my short-lived pot-smoking days.

That nothing-to-do bubble in Indiana was less protective than one might imagine. I've often thought had I gone to the University of Rhode Island, I might not have ever done anything rebellious, since partying was a way of life at big state schools. What grain would I have gone against in such a hedonistic place?

I gave my soul to a Taylor girl, a Christian Education major who gave me a considerably unchristian education. Rather than celebrate my enlightenment, I mourned the loss of my ignorant innocence, as well as the loss of the girl, who didn't last long at Taylor. She was an outsider, too, and that's what did me in. Perhaps your average college boy would be high-fiving fraternity brothers after conquering such a supple landscape, but I knew that it was me who'd been conquered, not her.

A few months after my heart had been broken, I met the highly acclaimed guitarist Phil Keaggy, who was playing a concert at nearby Marion College. Before the performance, a college buddy introduced me to Phil as a fellow musician. Phil suggested we jam, and a musical conversation ensued. After his performance, he told me that he thought someday we'd be in a band together. Three years later, this assumption or prophecy or wild guess, call it what you will, came true when I made the trek to Upstate New York and joined the Phil Keaggy Band. But that is another story.

The fantasy of becoming a working musician swirled inside my head while I continued my course at Taylor.

I had a philosophy teacher in my junior year named Herb Nygren, and it was he who opened up the world to me, and made faith intriguing. If there was a single thing that my college education gave me, it was the sense that spiritual exploration was not only interesting and entertaining, but necessary in order to stave off the crippling atrophy that seemed to make invalids of so many religious people, from Jesus' time to the present.

As I pondered my own beliefs, questioning God seemed to be a biblical expression of faith, and even worship. Searching for God would have to include a scrutinizing of Him in order for a mutual satisfaction to occur between Creator and creature. The tale of Jacob wrestling with God in the wilderness and limping away, the victor, suggested a picture of God Almighty wearing a "Question Authority" T-shirt, and saying "Bring it on" to honest doubters.

Evangelicals hammer away at the idea of a personal relationship with Christ, which I resonate with to this day. Yet, they depersonalize the concept with rigid theologies, particularly Calvinism, which foists a determined, willful God on hapless Christians who have no choice in the matter of following Him or Her. The notion of God choosing some for Heaven and some for Hell does not sound like the gracious Shepherd I heard about in Sunday school, going to the ends of the earth to find one lost sheep.

Calvinists, who often call themselves "Reformed," love the box they have created for God; in preparing this concrete place for Him, they sequester Him in finiteness and smugly declare the subservience of His love, a muted affection smothered and dwarfed and beneath a gargantuan Will which God's own tears cannot erode. Calvinism seems to be at home in the Midwest, as squared-off as a road map of Indianapolis.

The red clay on my southern soles doesn't blend with the dry dirt of the Midwest. My blood doesn't want to freeze, and my will doesn't want to roll over. Like midwesterners, I'm holding my ground, but it's a different kind of soil. This dirt tastes like it's been trodden upon by gospel singers, woman warriors, and spirit-filled portrait painters, with names like Sister Rosetta, Flannery O'Connor, and Howard Finster. The ground I'm holding is my faith, flexible and evolving, open and mystical, childlike and offensive. I don't want to put a name to my beliefs, lest they feel contrived or made-up.

May God Almighty recognize me apart from the labels I've acquired:

"gangstuh" (my mother's pronunciation)

sanguine

ENTJ

7 on the Enneagram

Yankee

lost

unteachable

Baptist
Catholic
not a Christian
conservative
liberal
apostate
...and forgive me for the labels I've bequeathed.

Meanwhile, my Southern Born Woman smiles and knows my type, but is content to call me baby, which is not a made-up name.

18

Graven Images

Soft and low, like a muffled bass drum, the canvas has a voice. I like stretching it across the pine slats, and firmly tacking it in place, mindful that the mesh pattern is square with the frame. After a coat or two of gesso, it has that sound, soft and low. I tap it with my fingertips, my ear held close as if listening to the heartbeat of an elk.

Music and art always competed for my heart, and I guess music won, but not without a fight.

When I enrolled in college as a wide-eyed freshman, I signed up as an art major. The art department was chaired by an interesting and odd person, whose birdlike nervousness betrayed a sensitive nature. A delicate soul with indelicate political views, Jack was the only person I've ever known to be a member of the John Birch Society.

Of course, Jack's viewpoints were not uncommon in Indiana in 1972, where billboards proclaiming "Get the US out of the UN" or "Register Communists, not firearms" were as common as cornfields. How ironic that, a decade later, his hero Ronald Reagan would slash government funding for the arts.

Politics aside, Jack was a sincere Christian, and although he was of the Fundamentalist stripe, he earnestly sought to understand and communicate with his flower child students, who seemed dichotomous to him.

As he was the chairman of the art department, and the primary painting professor, I still am amazed that Jack was color-blind. He would often point to one of his portraits in progress and ask students if the colors were "right." I admire his desire to be a realist, although he was encumbered by a lens that only made sense to him. His reality was just a bit different from everyone else's "norm." Forty years later, I find something curiously wonderful in that idea.

Nonetheless, I waited for Jack to take his sabbatical before I took any courses in painting.

Through a visiting professor whose name escapes me, I found a style contrary to my haphazard way of life. I painted in a definitive, almost paint-by-numbers, hard-edged motif, reducing images down to their most essential shapes and colors.

I still have some of these paintings, and while I like them, I now recognize the fear in them. Reducing a face to very few shade zones, much like a child's paint-by-number painting, was my way of ignoring the details while still making good art. I avoided the interplay of dark and light by reducing those infinite shades to one or the other. The paintings were essentially pop art, and I was proud of them, having distilled images down to their bare essence. Nowadays, I wonder if I would have been far more satisfied with these pop works if I'd been equally adept at some semblance of realism. None of my realistic work from that period enthralls me, while, admittedly, my hard-edged portraits of Truman Capote and bluesman Taj Mahal have places of honor on my walls.

Like my personality, my canvases were bold. As much as I like those assertive, confident paintings, I wonder if finding such a style not only pleased my palette for spice, but also averted attention from the fact that I wasn't all that disciplined in capturing the details realism demanded.

You can only paint by numbers so many times before it becomes boring, so after graduating from college, I painted a few more times, got married, and then lost interest. I kept my brushes and my paints, which eventually hardened in their metal tubes. The old blue tackle box, filled with brushes, paints, and linseed oil, followed the course of my life, always settling underneath basement stairs or the bottom shelf of a utility closet, unopened for over twenty-five years. My heart was like one of those dried-up tubes of paint; blue, most likely.

Not too long ago, I heard that familiar, soft and low bass drum sound, and found myself in step with its beat.

It started on a beach. My Southern Born Woman and I were relaxing under a wide, blue umbrella one sunny, scenic afternoon. Reaching into her handbag for a book, she handed me a small set of watercolors and a pad. I drew the yellow and gray beach house that perched over her right shoulder, as I listened to her read from Barbara Brown Taylor's *Gospel Medicine*.

Then, I turned my attention to my reader, a reluctant subject, and painted her relaxed, graceful form reclining in a blue beach chair, her beauty crowned with a ball cap.

Not long after that, I went on my first tour with Emmylou Harris, and along with a few books, I took a set of watercolors and a pad of postcard stock.

Our first stop was Monterey, California. On a beautiful May afternoon, I walked along a pathway above the Pacific, photographing flowers and scenery. When I returned to my room, I wrote a poem to my Dearest Companion, and adorned it with detailed paintings of the flowers. Something stirred me, like a paint stick awakening a bucket of paralyzed paint.

Our next stop was less quaint, but I was determined to find something worthy to paint.

I made a vow that I would search for beauty, no matter how bland the landscape or how dreary the surroundings. I would photograph my findings, and return to my hotel room, and begin to paint. As a way to keep my eye objective, I would often turn the image in my computer upside-down, which would force me to paint what I was actually seeing; right-side up, I might find myself painting what I thought I saw. Oh, I'm not that clever; it's a time-proven trick painters have employed for years.

In a gray-skied Kansas outpost, between two old abandoned buildings, I discovered a small Japanese garden. As long as my inner eye was open, finding something to paint was easy.

That year, the band traveled the United States, Canada, and Europe, and my paint box and camera were my quiet companions. The solace that I experienced was soothing, and for the first time in all my years of being a touring musician, the hotel room television was left off.

Back in Nashville, my Dearest Companion started receiving postcards or envelopes adorned with my findings—houseboats in Vancouver, a taco truck in Portland, a canal in Amsterdam, votive candles in a London cathedral, and serpentine steeples from Copenhagen. Her favorite from that season is a white cat walking across the top of a chair at an outdoor café in Brussels.

These small paintings, the size of an index card, are detailed and emotional, unlike the large, loud, hard-edged paintings of my youth. As she and I find so much commonality in art and literature, it's a fitting offering to send my woman; a postcard of my own making, telling her the obvious without so many words, and certainly nicer than a "Greetings from Des Moines" photo montage.

Working on such a small scale is somehow soothing, and the finish line is attainable. There is a performance art quality in this process, a perceived drama, as the card makes its journey from somewhere on a map to Nashville, Tennessee. Nearly every card I've dropped in a mailbox has made its destination, like a homing pigeon that knows where it's supposed to go. The cards arrive slightly tattered and weathered, with various official markings from where they've come. Some artists finish a painting by putting a coat of varnish on it; I finish mine by affixing a stamp to it and pushing it through a mail slot.

The postcard paintings are part of my touring routine. Once I'm home, I resort to other means of creativity.

Off the road, which is most of the time, I always have a canvas, stretched and waiting, on my easel in what is supposed to be my breakfast room. Sometimes it will sit for days, white as a ghost. Sometimes I'm inspired to paint; often I will paint to be inspired.

When I was working on folkie Ralston Bowles's recording, he stayed at my home. I rarely have clients stay with me, but he's an old friend, and it was my pleasure to host him, as well as to record him. I warned him, though, that after recording together for ten hours each day, we might want a quiet break from each other when the evenings came.

At the end of the second day of recording, he sat in my breakfast nook talking. I think the chemotherapy treatments coursing their way through his veins had brought on a surge of verbosity, so I stood in the room, exhausted, wondering how to find the needed break without hurting anyone's feelings. I finally said, "Sit down, and keep talking," and began painting his portrait as he spoke. It now hangs in his home in Grand Rapids.

One of the most difficult things about painting on a larger scale is realizing when the painting is finished. When can you let go and sign your name? One of my paintings is abstract, meaningless as far as I know. Letting go and finding beauty in the shapes and colors and technique took some doing. Yet, somehow, I find what I've done to be agreeable, pleasing to the eye, and filling me with a sense of accomplishment.

I understand the concept of the eye needing to find pleasure. As a child I would demand the blue plate, among the several choices in our everyday china. This brought my siblings and parents endless amusement, as I would invariably be handed the green or the red plate. It's hard to believe I was ever that obsessive, but apparently, I was. My eye still finds immense pleasure in all things blue, although my mother no longer has those colored dishes.

I think of my old color-blind professor asking students if he'd gotten the tone of a face right, not having experienced optical pleasure for himself, but hoping to succeed in bringing it beyond his own understanding.

What makes a combination of colors soothing and satisfying? Why do some sequences of notes and tones please the ear while others seem random and meaningless, if not dissonant and unpleasant? Why does the ear know the difference between the soulful lullaby of a loving mother and the nagging drone of a dissatisfied customer?

Is this discernment our Creator's DNA flowing through our minds and spirits? Perhaps the urge to create and the ability to objectively evaluate what we hear, read, see, smell, taste, etc., comes from some primeval place, something beyond education and experience, yet from the very same place that spurs us to become adventurous and enlightened.

Or maybe the creative process just comes down to one person letting another know "I'm alive!"

I am thinking of my scratched, blue tackle box with its hardened paint tubes and forgotten brushes, and how the lack of a soulmate rusted the hinges on that old case. When love came to me, the urge to create goodness, and the desire to please another's eye, oiled my creative engine. My heart opened slowly, like the first time I opened an old blue tackle box in twenty-five years.

And now it's beating, like an elk's.

19

Maw-tucket

I'm thinking about thankfulness.

This quotation from G. K. Chesterton is something I might apply more heartily to my good life:

"You say grace before meals. All right. But I say grace before the concert and the opera, and grace before the play and pantomime, and grace before I open a book, and grace before sketching, painting, swimming, fencing, boxing, walking, playing, dancing and grace before I dip the pen in the ink."

Summer 1974, I was home in Rhode Island, trying to earn a little money before heading back to Taylor University for my junior year. I got a job at Hasbro, the toy manufacturer in Pawtucket, Rhode Island.

It's pronounced *Puh-tucket*, by the way. I remember when the Pawtucket Red Sox came to play the Nashville Sounds some years back, and a Sounds fan was jeering at the boys from Rhode Island.

"Hey Paw-tucket! Where's Maw-tucket?" I guess it could have been worse.

Pawtucket is an industrial city just north of Providence. The Industrial Revolution in America started there with Slater's Mill. Samuel Slater was born in Belper, Derbyshire, a stone's throw from the site of the Three Horseshoes Pub, a place that revolutionized my heart and soul. But that's another story.

Two centuries ago, Slater memorized the technological details of England's textile industry, and effectively ushered New England into its financial heyday, creating knitting mills all over Rhode Island and Massachusetts. He started life as an indentured apprentice and ended it as a wealthy industrialist.

By the 1970s, the main industry of Pawtucket was the Hasbro Toy Company. Home for the summer, I discovered Hasbro was hiring.

I was working the second shift, 4:00 p.m. to 11:00 p.m., on an assembly line making accessories for the popular G.I. Joe dolls. For a vocal opponent of the Vietnam War, it was an ironic job to have, making weapons of mass destruction for G.I. Joe, with his popular kung fu grip.

Aware of the irony, I went home one night and sat at my mother's grand piano, and wrote a Christmas ballad called "G.I. Joe," about all the little children who'd be receiving him and his accessories on the birthday of the Prince of Peace. It was a nod to two of my heroes, Jesus and Randy Newman.

Now, *there's* a pair.

My job was to drill a hole and insert a screw into a piece of plastic, the end product of which I can't remember. It was the worst job on the assembly line, not quite enough work for two people, but a little too much for one. The conveyor belt would bring gray pieces of plastic to me faster than I could send them along to the next person, and before I knew it, I was backed up and buried by these nondescript parts.

Most of the people on the line were speaking Portuguese, and only they and God Almighty knew what they were yelling at me, although I had a pretty good idea. Eventually, the line supervisor would come to my aid, inserting the screws while I vigorously drilled holes. It was endless and futile. Alas, I was not in the same echelon as Rosie the Riveter.

After my first shift at the new job, I went home discouraged.

I couldn't imagine surviving a summer of being the slowest drone at Hasbro. Here I was, a college-educated, well-traveled, and privileged young man, being humbled by immigrants who had a way with plastic.

I told my parents that I didn't think I could last for long; that either I'd give up on Hasbro or Hasbro would give up on me. Either way, I'd be a Hasbro has-been.

My mother suggested that I read a book by a Pentecostal preacher named Merlin Carothers. I cringed, naturally. I've been cringing for many years now, with the book suggestions from dear old Mom. "Have you read the John Stott devotional I bawt you fuh Chrismiss yet? I sent one to the president; I wunduh if he's read it."

It's hard enough finding time to read the books I want to read, never mind the ones she thinks I should read. However, on this hot summer night, reflecting on a summer of futile hole-drilling, I was desperate enough to give some consideration to my mother's literary suggestions.

Reading a book by a Pentecostal would be a stretch, but the name Merlin must have softened me to the idea. Maybe some deep magic was at work. After all, a guy named Merlin can't be all bad.

The book was called *From Prison to Praise*, just one of many "Praise" titles the good Merlin had written in his literary career. Merlin's magic spell was really a scripture verse: In all things give thanks. He believed one should literally thank God for everything in one's life, no matter how terrible those things were.

He would cite story after story of people whose difficult lives were transformed by thankfulness. Torn-up lives would somehow be restored by the resolute speaking of the words "thank you"; practitioners of this rite would often move from the worst of circumstances to the best.

I'm sure Merlin was praising God Almighty all the way to the bank.

Nonetheless, it remains a radical idea, doesn't it?

The belief that God is involved with the details of our lives raises more questions than it provides answers. Something good happens to me and I say "Thank God"; maybe I just missed getting broadsided by a drunk driver, or maybe I just made a killing in song-writing royalties. "Glory to God in the highest!" But then the person who *did* get broadsided comes to mind, and, on the one hand, "Thank God it was him not me," but on the other... Is the victim's family saying "Thank God"? If I could understand the ways of God, I suppose I'd *be* God.

I like Steve Earle's statement, "I just believe there's a God, and it ain't me, and that's about as far as I've gotten."

Dreadful things can happen in this world of ours, things that make us feel so far from God Almighty's care, things that make existentialism seem palatable. The idea that God is involved in the details has always been with me; I was raised with it. As a bald man, I chuckle at the scripture verse "He numbers the hairs on my head." No big deal, Lord.

Of course, my Dearest Companion reminds me that the saying is actually "The Devil is in the details."

Well, damn.

Thinking about a summer on the assembly line, I had few options.

So, there I sat reading Merlin's story after story about miserable circumstances shifting in the light of the words "Thank you." And I was miserable enough at my Hasbro workbench to begin meditating on the praise of God Almighty. I started my second day on the second shift with a will to thank God for my job. For the next seven hours, I kept my mind busy with the words "Thank you, Jesus." It is an odd remembrance, the willful occupation of my thoughts with the goodness of God, because, frankly, I've GDed unpleasant situations more than not. I say this not with pride, but as a matter of fact. I'm not some stellar Christian with a Sola Gloria attitude.

Back at the drill press, with the praise of God repeating silently in my mind, nothing seemed to change. The concrete floor didn't get any more comfortable under my Converse All Stars. I didn't get any faster and the conveyor belt didn't slow down. The gray plastic pieces would start crowding up as workers down the line tapped their fingers. In my mind, I thought, *Well, this is ridiculous, but thank you, Lord, that I'm in a job I'm unsuited for, and that it's not going great.*

Whether it was Providence or just Industry watching out for itself, my patient supervisor would come to my aid and catch me up with the assembly line. *It must be working*, I thought, and I'd keep on thanking.

Friday morning came with a new job offer from a man at Dad's church—Bob Glover. I was offered the job of a laborer for the construction firm that Bob was a foreman for. *God be praised*, I could kiss Hasbro good-bye, and I did. I can't remember, but I probably didn't even bother showing up for the second shift to say, "You can't fire me, I quit!" I was happy to move on, and of course, I thanked God, and decided that Merlin's spell worked.

I enjoyed working construction so much that it never occurred to me to continue my newfound rite of thankfulness. It was as if the words "Thank you" were a spell that I no longer needed. (It would seem that we learn little from good outcomes, although I would hope that's not really true. Perhaps with some reflection, my lesson has become clear after three decades of cloudiness on the subject.)

I recently read, and unfortunately can't remember where, that God is well-suited to receive praise. It isn't neediness that causes the Almighty to desire our thanks; but perhaps it's just as simple as God's *deservedness*. When we narrowly escape from the speeding car, to whom else do we give our gratitude, whether an Almighty Hand was involved or not? The life God gives us continues for another sunrise, another day of enjoying the beauty of the earth, of enjoying the companionship of friends, and another day to bask in the delirium of love.

Back on the assembly line, where nothing seemed any different, perhaps the most unlikely of changes was indeed occurring, the slight smoothing over of the rocky terrain of my own heart.

And if that's the case, may wonders never cease.

20

Love Inn

Sometimes I wonder if my cross to bear is believing in Christ while running from His people. I'm always trying to figure out why He'd want to socialize with them in the first place. The Gospel story doesn't have Jesus enjoying a drink with the scribes and Pharisees: More often than not, He's enjoying the company of shysters, hookers, and a multitude of people whose lives have gone flat wrong. One rarely reads of Him enjoying Judea's religious *right*.

I can't picture Jesus enjoying the company of any of the preachers I see on TV, can you? Pandering know-it-alls who've figured Him out—why would He want to bother? Lord knows, it wouldn't be for the pasteurized grape juice. The men He called to be disciples were fishermen, thick-skinned tough guys, and politically incorrect zealots who probably didn't enjoy the company of lawyers and priests any more than Jesus did.

I realize that my inference is that, of course, *I* would be the Christian Jesus would want to share a bottle with. I can dream, can't I?

In my line of work, just the word "Christian" evokes negative feelings and fear; assumptions are easily made. A while back, I was producing a singer who told me that I was one of two decent Christians he knew; the rest repelled him. He was an atheist, left-wing, and Jewish, and outspokenly anti-Christian. I took issue with his set of prejudices, and he confessed that I was onto something, yet remained unmoved in his opinions, at times being downright insensitive and rude. "It's these fuckin' Christians," he'd say, when agitated about politics or just about anything. Apart from his immense talent and his charm, he was really no different from your average Fundamentalist spouting off about who controls the media, or who's a communist, but he didn't see the point.

His rationale for not believing in God was that he believed there was "something bigger behind it all," to which I said, "Yeah, what if that's God?" All of this was truly in good fun. We made some great records together, despite the chasm between our philosophies of life. Like me, he had run up against a few of God Almighty's worst sales reps; I didn't hold God responsible, and he did.

I've experienced just about every kind of Christian denomination one could dream up. I've always noticed that the church name always emphasizes the very quality that is found lacking at that particular oasis. Want to find a good place for fellowship? It won't be at a place called Springfield Community Church. In need of mercy? Avoid a place called Grace Church.

I'm somewhat of a bedridden Episcopalian most Sunday mornings, but the cup I occasionally drink from is served downtown at Christ Cathedral. After many years of Protestantism's informalities, the idea of rendezvousing with the Spirit through poetry, music, readings, and silent, poignant gestures makes sense to me, particularly given the haphazard life I live.

Standing in this beautiful building, I like the sound of my Dearest Companion's voice quietly singing the Sanctus, and reciting the Creed with a whispered certainty. Sometimes, I lean a little closer so that I can hear her voice over mine, close enough to feel her inhaling and exhaling the breath of God.

Strange as it may sound from an extrovert, one thing I like about going to the cathedral is that few people know me. There I have no notoriety, no voice, no activity, and no responsibilities. I recite the prayers, cross myself, receive the Eucharist from a priest who didn't know my name until recently, and quietly leave without giving my soul to anyone but God Almighty.

It's taken me a long time to finally figure out that being known is a liability in most religious circles. I like being a stranger in the strange land of Christendom, particularly when I consider some of the bizarre congregations I've exposed my bluesman's heart to.

The best of the worst was a church called Love Inn, far up in the frozen North of New York State. You'd think the name alone would have sent me running, but I had good reason to wind up there.

After I met Phil Keaggy during my Taylor years, we continued corresponding about music, life, and God. During those years of letter writing, Phil and his new bride, Bernadette, moved from the Midwest to Ithaca, New York, to join the counterculture Christian church called Love Inn.

The possibility of being in a working band continued to dominate my waking dreams.

Love Inn was started by a disk jockey named Scott Ross, who had hobnobbed with the Beatles, the Rolling Stones, and Dylan in the sixties. He was married to Nedra Talley, one of the Ronettes, who had a huge hit with "Be My Baby." The two of them converted to the Christian faith in what was probably a remarkable Damascus Road experience, and left the glamour for Upstate New York, and the barn that eventually became Love Inn.

The upside of Love Inn was that it strove to be on the edge, creatively speaking. Theater, dance, music, and art were vital to this group of young Christians. The opportunity to be among creative people of faith was exciting.

In the summer preceding my senior year of college, I visited the Keaggys and Love Inn in Ithaca, New York. While I was there, Phil said that I needed to have an interview with one of his "shepherds" at the church. While it struck me as odd that this was a necessity, I wanted to be a good guest, and I was also intrigued with the idea of communal Christian living.

I was interviewed by a young man I will call "Rock," who was in his late twenties. He was both giddy and stern for the Lord. He asked why I had come to Love Inn, and I replied that I was there to visit my friend Phil.

Wrong answer.

I scrambled for the right answer, which was something like "I want to grow closer to God." *Poor God Almighty must get sick of having His or Her name dragged into awkward situations like this.*

I told Rock about my girlfriend E, who was not a Christian. "Brother," he said, "if you were a member of our church, you would not be allowed to be unequally yoked." I replied that E didn't have a problem with Jesus, but that she didn't yet understand that she didn't have to change in order to follow Him. I suggested that her process of finding God wouldn't be via an instantaneous conversion, but would more likely be akin to an orphan girl being wooed by a handsome prince. It would take time for her to believe in the reality of Love.

Again, *wrong answer.*

At this point, Rock said, "I don't believe you know Jesus at all," which was stunning news to me.

As if to confirm his suspicions I responded eloquently, "Shit."

Keaggy came to my aid, earnestly proclaiming that I was indeed a believer. But the damage was done. There would be no convincing Rock that I was among the Chosen.

A few days later, I drove back to Rhode Island with no idea that one day I would find myself between a hard place and a man called Rock.

Following my graduation from college, Phil invited me to come to Love Inn to play keyboards for him. It was hard to resist the offer, knowing that I would be playing alongside one of the best of the best.

Having met Phil's rhythm guitarist Lynn Nichols, a man with an indomitable sense of humor, I was ready for some camaraderie and music making. I moved there with a sense of excitement, open to the idea of this new form of Christianity.

Love Inn's belief system was based upon the premise that God would speak to individuals through elders we called "shepherds," and that His will for lowly sheep like me was to "submit" to them. It's no wonder that the church was an old barn, with all these "sheep" running about.

It seems so foolish now, but my willingness to explore this brand of Christianity was aligned with my genuine quest for intimacy with God. I wanted depth, growth, change, revolution in my heart and soul. (I still do.)

Instead, what I encountered was a group of "elders," all in their late twenties and early thirties, who wanted to know every detail of my life, no matter how private. These were not trained ministers, nor were they theologically astute, but their ability to be Yes Men had led them as far up the pyramid as they could go.

The lessons I'd learned from my overly involved mother and grandmother should have been enough to send me running from this crowd, but the sound of Phil's Les Paul guitar coming through a Fender Deluxe amplifier drowned out the screaming angel on my shoulder.

One of my most disturbing memories was when Rock summoned the elders into our band's practice room to confront Phil about what he perceived as a lethargic attitude toward "the Lord's work."

Phil sat silently as the elders proceeded to take him to task, trying to get to the bottom of what was ailing him. He had nothing to say.

I had only been at Love Inn for a week or two when this incident took place, so I wasn't sure what the protocol was. But I found myself suddenly overwhelmed with tears, sobbing.

"What is it, brother?" Scott asked. When I could finally collect myself, I reminded these pious "elders" that only two weeks before, Phil's wife, Bernadette, had miscarried a baby who was only two months shy of being born. I was incredulous, and asked, "What do you expect? They've lost their baby!" The elders admitted that perhaps I was onto something, and left us alone.

This scenario was typical of the mind-policing that went on at Love Inn.

Every detail of my life was subject to inquiry. Rock wanted to know the most minute details of my finances, whether or not I kept my room clean, and everything short of asking if I was regular. My earnest quest for spiritual intimacy led me to allow for the daily discomfort of spiritual cavity searches by the God squad from Hell.

As a member of this weird little church, being on the road was the best place I could be, away from the daily grind of our very insulated body of fanatics. I was with friends, playing music, enjoying the road, and sharing a few glasses every night, just like the Willie Nelson song talks about.

The band we formed was an outreach of the church, traveling the country, encouraging believers, and playing innovative music. When I consider that the mission of our band was revival, it's ironic that our sound had more in common with the Grateful Dead than with a gospel group.

Of course, the powers that be had sent Rock out on the road with us, a spy posing as a sound technician, cracking the whip and trying to somehow snuff out the flame of joy that we were able to maintain. Fate or God Almighty had a sick sense of humor in linking me once again to Rock, the man who was sure that I didn't know Jesus.

Rock was incapable of finding humor in any situation, which naturally made his delegated position of Babysitter to the Band a difficult one for him and us. Inevitably, he discovered in me a project, someone he needed to change for the glory of God Almighty. Like the matriarchs who found in me a similar challenge, Rock was, well, a real mother.

As was the case in my family of origin, in my new tribe of choice I was the Funny Guy.

To Rock, humorless and grim, I wasn't holy enough or serious enough, and to make matters worse, I was smitten with E, who wasn't a member of Love Inn. By the time I had moved there, she had embraced Christianity, and was a student at nearby Syracuse University. When she became engaged to me, no one at Love Inn exhibited the usual delight upon seeing the simple ring I'd bought her. Their glazed Stepford eyes stared blankly, and plastic smiles turned up with effort, and I reluctantly knew I was seeing trouble ahead.

Instead of congratulatory remarks for our engagement, we were told, "It will be good to talk about." I sensed that this was euphemistic for "We have other plans for you, and there's nothing you can do about it," but said nothing to E about my feelings of dread. (Years later, I would realize that saying nothing to her about my feelings wasn't a good idea.)

Meanwhile, Rock's giant eye seemed to follow me wherever I went. His rigid hand would try to brush aside any joyous declaration of love I would make, making my engagement something of a trial instead of a sweet season of transition. His paradigm of the way things should be would not allow for variation, and it was clear that it was either his way or the highway.

Rock forever ruined the word "brother" for me, because it always preceded a harshly placed word, meant to push my tiller in a direction that my small boat didn't wish to go. His cruel and uncaring manner was a part of the process; it was a boot camp for the Lord, and he was my drill sergeant. I wanted to go over his head in this oddly organized hierarchy of men, but when I assessed the situation, I knew it was best to keep silence.

The one time I did suggest to Scott, the main honcho, that I didn't think Rock understood me, and perhaps there was someone else who could "shepherd" me, I was harshly rebuked. "You wanna follow me? You follow him!" (By the way, the word "rebuke" was a highly charged word in this particular circle. It was imbued with a sense of spirituality, implied discernment, and condescension. When someone *rebuked* you, it was serious, akin to being triple-dog-dared in the movie *A Christmas Story.*)

Rock's only glimmer of joy seemed to be in the proclamation of this strange concoction of bad theology and religious hierarchy, whose advocates literally referred to what they practiced as "the Government of God." Of course he'd be ecstatic about it; he had some of the power and out on the road, he answered to no one.

We played our music and sang our songs, but Rock was the one who was entrusted with the enlightened message, a new improved version of Christianity. He would take the stage before we did, and introduce us as "men who had earned the right to speak," as if our giving up our right to protest, think, or differ with his opinion was a pleasing thing to God. The audience rarely cared; they just wanted to hear the amazing Phil Keaggy practice his magic.

Rock was yet another representative of God Almighty who didn't make sense to me, who made me want to flee from all of Christendom. I think the only thing that kept me from doing so was the image of God Almighty that my father's life had so beautifully manifested. Dad was the polar opposite of God's unholy scourge, Rock. Like a child who knows the difference between good touch and bad touch, I quickly learned the difference between those who lived to serve and those who lived to *be* served.

Thirty-odd years later, I occasionally see a few remaining friends from those days of touring, all of whom reside and work in the Nashville music community. We were brought together in that crucible of craziness, and have remained bonded by its white-hot fire. Occasionally, over a good bottle of red, we'll remind each other about our days of keeping one eye open for our elder Rock. Now, we laugh and shake our heads, wondering what God had to do with any of it.

It amazes me that the hierarchy was such that a group of grown men would cower before such an unreasonable taskmaster as Rock, but some moments are hard to explain, and most battles don't get fought, even if they might be worth it.

Not long ago, Lynn Nichols asked why the band never thought to leave Love Inn and do business on our own. I attributed our paralysis to the dark magic conjured up when people possess power over others. We were afraid of what would happen if we breathed some outside oxygen.

Once, we were playing in a place called Philippi, West Virginia, high on a mountain, in a beautiful venue that looked out into the hills. We were having a particularly good evening of music, and I took a moment to publicly acknowledge our crew. I pointed to Ben Pearson, who came out from behind a stack of speakers, and told the crowd that he was the hardest-working roadie in the business. Then I pointed to Rock, who stood behind the audio console in the audience. I said, "Please give our soundman Rock a hand."

After the concert, we all partook in the backbreaking task of loading our equipment onto the truck. Rock, with his ever-present snorkel-hood shielding his great square head, approached me angrily and yelled, "Brother, don't you EVER call me the soundman again! I'm the fucking producer!"

I couldn't win.

Ah, thank you, Jesus. May I have another?

That same year, we were at a Shell station in Ypsilanti, Michigan, surrounded by walls of snow, preparing to fill the tanks of our two vehicles. No one knew where the key to the truck's gas cap was, and we obviously needed fuel. Rock's trademark impatience gave way, and he pried it off with a crowbar, disgusted with whichever of us had been so careless as to lose the key, yet himself being so careless as to ruin the gas cap and rip the filler neck.

Later, in our hotel room, Ben put his hands in his pocket and said,

"Oh, no," as he pulled the key from his trousers. I told him to flush it down the toilet, but he dutifully went to Rock and confessed his guilt.

Over a beer, I recently asked him about that night. He remembers it, as I do, like it was yesterday. He laughed about my insistence that he flush the key down the toilet, amazed by the notion that perhaps God would've ratted him out if he hadn't confessed.

And then he related another vignette that will remain his story, about having his spirit crushed one too many times by our tormentor. "That was the night that I called my mother and asked for her credit card number; I had had it, and was going to catch a bus back home." Slightly moved, Ben went on, "But it was you guys—you and Keaggy and Lynn—I felt like I couldn't leave my pals alone in a bad situation."

We were a small squad of men led by someone who wanted to put us in harm's way, but at least we had each other. That was thirty-five years ago, and all I have left to show for my time at Love Inn is those three guys. And that's more than I bargained for.

Love Inn's twisted psychology of pretending to be God's Voice in my life never took full root, yet when I went against it, I felt a sense of foreboding and fear that I had never experienced before. I didn't want to make God or Rock or Love Inn mad.

I knew the end of my tenure at Love Inn would arrive; the translucent remarks were telltale signs and omens, black clouds, with the theme from *Jaws* quietly playing underneath it all. The Government of God was ruled by tyrants, and I was just waiting it out. Soothed by our band's music, I endured the oddness, and continued playing keyboards on the *Titanic*, partaking as little of this peculiar Eucharist as was possible.

When E and I announced our wedding date to our friend Phil Keaggy, his knee-jerk advice was "Don't tell Rock!" He knew what the cost of discipleship would be.

Word of our pending nuptials eventually reached the elders, who called an emergency meeting. A wedding date? This was indeed serious business. Something had to be done.

The elders told me that they not only wanted to choose the date for me, but possibly even the woman. My finding love and acting upon it without the involvement of God's Government was an insult to the entire process of *submission* and *discipleship*, the two most often intoned mantras of Love Inn.

Something had to give, apparently me.

And so, in a long, drawn-out, torturous fashion, I was asked to choose between love and Love Inn. The choice was easy, but the consequences were not. Leaving the band and the friendships therein was difficult, but I had to trust my own heart, and all else be damned. Luckily, the friendships that mattered to me within that small circle survived and continue to this day.

Going against the grain simply was not done at Love Inn, and I was excommunicated from the fellowship. I was told I could continue with the band for six months of concerts, but couldn't participate in church services or "family meetings." I knew I'd done the right thing for myself, and that I was running toward God Almighty, but psychologically, I felt as if I were running *from* him. The transition from cult member back to the World was one of the few times in my life when I've experienced depression and true loneliness.

But glory be, I finally got back to the real world.

When my new wife and I had our first fight, the first thought in my head was, "The elders were right." And many years later, when our marriage crumbled like a stale Communion wafer, I pictured Rock, the unbending representative of an unmerciful God, nodding "I told you so."

It bears saying that Scott Ross eventually left Love Inn and apologized to many folks, including me, for the errors of his youthful zeal. I stay in touch with him to this day. I know of no other former elders of Love Inn having had enough humility or self-awareness to own up to any former sheep. I wish them well.

About twenty years ago, I called Rock up from Nashville, ostensibly to say hello. We spoke for an awkward moment or two, and that was that. I knew that I was trying to forgive him, perhaps even desperately so, and I also knew that I couldn't complete the transaction without an apology. Through a casual conversation, I hoped to give him an easy threshold through which to carry what I imagined to be a burden for him.

I was wrong. Ministers often seem to be the least vulnerable, least confessional souls to walk the planet, at least those for whom being right is an idol.

This is the shape of unforgiveness—a chapter dedicated to an old nemesis, a chapter that has no happy ending, or at least none that will come in this lifetime.

The poison in some Communion cups is strong indeed.

21

The Church of Saint Johnny

Timing is everything. Two weeks before Christmas 2003, I told E I was leaving. We hobbled through the holidays with our secret weighing us down, our children unaware that all was about to change forever.

We waited until our fir tree was less than evergreen, shedding its sticky needles onto the living room rug, and on the worst day of our lives, we told them it was over. I will leave the details of that terrible evening in the sanctuaries of my daughters' and their parents' collective memory. Despite their acceptance of our divorce as "the best thing," the pain it caused my daughters is something I will regret forever.

I moved out a day or two before New Year's Eve. My friend Steve came over and helped me strap a bed onto the roof of my old Mercedes wagon. We brought it, along with my trusty Lowden guitar and a small TV, to the apartment. Steve helped me set up the bed, and then left.

I sat on the bare mattress and wept.

I wept for my children. I wept with the same uncertainty I knew they were feeling. What was to become of us? What lay ahead of us? I wept, my soul knowing more than I was conscious of, knowing that I was about to unearth feelings that I had shoved into the furthest corners of my worn-down heart. I wept, hoping God Almighty would have mercy on me, and receive my tears as a bitter, salty, early Passover offering, while wondering if He might forget me.

That evening, I went to a party at the Capitol Grille, hosted by my friends John and Natasha. Originally, I had planned on bringing E, but now all had changed, so I brought my old friend Dennis instead. We sat among John's coworkers, dining on Kobe steaks and drinking copious amounts of cabernet. Exuberantly happy, I finally went back to my little apartment and wrapped myself in the swaddling purple sheets of my single man's queen-sized bed.

I don't often remember my dreams, although when accompanied by a few glasses of red wine, they seem more insistent on being recognized. Shamans, prophets, seers, and soothsayers all place stock in the nocturnal playground of the subconscious. With all the noise that accompanies consciousness, perhaps there's something to the idea of the Spirit finding a wider berth in the vessel of our dreams.

Dehydrated, I woke at 3:00 a.m. My thirst had interrupted a dream that was fresh and vivid. My mind had taken me on a boat ride with the ghost of Johnny Cash sitting in the stern and dispensing homespun wisdom to me as I rowed across a choppy sea.

Knowing there was something in the phrase "the ghost of Johnny Cash," I immediately rose, found my laptop, and began writing a lyric. Eventually the verses I wrote would become a song, but in the wee hours they mirrored the image of my small craft getting obscured by the giant waves of my difficult choices.

I was a man who was cut in half, broken but believing, and somehow newly set free, although being set adrift was the true feeling of what looked to some like freedom. In my marriage, I felt no embrace clinging to me in love, and now I felt none either, but I hoped that the arms of God Almighty were wrapping around me as I descended into the abyss.

I needed that vision of Johnny on that old January night.

Johnny was someone I could relate to, a broken screw-up who had no pretensions. There were no skeletons in his closet; they were out in the open, lounging about his Tennessee home like old rivals and lovers at a reunion, awkwardness be damned. Of all the ghosts I could've dreamt of, thank God it was Johnny.

Johnny sat in the low end of my little boat, where the water splashes easily over the sides and into the hull, and where the bilge settles if you don't bail. My hands were raw, and my feet were getting cold and wet, but with Johnny singing hymns and cursing the wind, I knew I wasn't alone on my perilous journey.

Sometimes, I find myself in ancient places of worship, with statues of saints staring through me as if I'm not there. Stained-glass windows hold images of the holy in heavy solder borders, immovable and motionless, unreachable, although many people whisper prayers to them. Some of these saints lived their lives in near-perfect holiness, sacrificially carving out the Name of an Incarnate God into the heart of the church. Yet, I've never been inclined to whisper a petition to one of these images, no matter how beautiful and perfect it might be. I'm too busy trying to carve *my* name into the heart of God.

If I were to build a cathedral to the glory of God Almighty, the saints in residence would be like the Man in Black. The sun would shine through cracked glass images that I could brush my fingers against with a sense of recognition, as if looking at photographs of my ancestors. Statues wouldn't stand in holy poses, but would bend under the weight of burdens and failures, looking parishioners dead in the eye, smiling a crooked grin.

In my heart's cathedral, there is a floating stained-glass window, where Saint Johnny sits in the stern of a rowboat as the sea rages around him. He's ailing and wild-eyed like John the Baptist in the Old West. His halo tilts like a ragged porkpie hat, and his feet are covered with salt water. He knows where he's been, does he ever, and his eyes are on the horizon.

Johnny is all the saint I need to get to where I'm going.

22

The Letter Box

Consider the interplay between heart, mind, and history.

The remembrance of a moment, or even of a lifetime, is at once solid, fluid, and vaporous. Forgotten, then suddenly recalled, a waiting ember suddenly bursting into flame, stoked by a random scent of lemon, a sudden gust, cyan blue on a book's dust jacket, a sequence of notes, or the sound of a syllable falling from a moist mouth.

My thoughts turn to my ex-wife. E and I have never compared how our history looks through the dingy windows of individual recollection, but I'm quite sure we have different stories, both right and both wrong. The lens of remembrance has many functions—distortion, diffusion, outright denial, focus, accuracy, acceptance. So much of how we remember a story is wrapped up in what we need the story to give us at the moment of its telling.

The story of our failed marriage was important to me, especially in the context of having to explain it to the religious people in my life. While I told no lies to my priest, my mother, church friends, and others, my religion made me feel the pressure to disclose the details. I found myself having to justify ending the marriage under guidelines defined by the Bible. Yet, had the authorities found no such justification, I would have nonetheless carried on with the dismantling of our life as we knew it.

Many of us like to be regaled with the details of failure. It is human nature to desire inappropriate intimacy, hence the shady viewing of what our eyes can do without, the leaning into the hot and hushed whisper of gossip, and the lingering aftertaste of delicious poison.

In retrospect, I wish I had hidden the story deep within the well of tears it had created. Some who heard me out eventually agreed that my departure was justified. It pains me now that their opinions mattered at all, but I understand from whence I've come, and I, too, have sat in the judgment seat, and pondered the wisdom and validity of others who took this radical course before I did.

In the light of approval, I suppose my defensive id felt affirmed, but my weary bluesman's heart felt that the carcass of our marriage was being picked over and examined in some sort of holy roller autopsy with my priest, my mother, my friends and ex-friends all in attendance.

What seemed true to me was that I was an unloved man. Indeed, I was, and that had been the state of things for so long that I came to believe that it had always been so.

A few years after my divorce, I decided to clean out my garage. This is a lofty, unachievable goal that I would annually attempt. I had a two-car garage, but it had been only within the last couple of years that I'd been able to fit a car into it. My garage was full of outdated recording gear, drums, guitar amplifiers, and barely used gardening tools, all of which made me feel like I was parking in a pawnshop.

On this particular day of cleaning, I was sidetracked by a large box. The box held several smaller boxes, and one of them was filled with letters from Dad, Mom, my siblings, my grandmother, and old friends I'd forgotten about or lost track of. I scanned a few of my dad's letters, and set them aside to read another day. I threw everything else into the trash.

There was a lone shoebox left in the large box; it was decorated with a serene camping scene, implying that the sporty moccasins within would lead my feet into something more inviting than the wilderness they eventually walked into.

I removed the lid, and saw the unmistakable handwriting of my ex-wife. Her pen hand was steady and consistent, always producing perfectly printed letters, minute and artful. They revealed the care and thoughtfulness with which she wrote her words, ponderous and deliberate, exact and delicate.

Most were dated from the seventies, when our relationship began. There were others from the eighties, and fewer and fewer, perhaps none from the nineties.

She was a woman of few words, perhaps acutely aware of their power, perhaps even more aware of the power of silence. She said little without weighing and analyzing, risking or committing. She was endowed with great restraint when it came to words, rarely speaking out of turn, never gossiping, and never revealing her hand, perhaps out of both wisdom and fear.

If one's strength, stamina, and will are measured by the ability to keep silence, then E is the strongest person I have ever met. She is also a person of character and good nature.

And so it was that I found myself in a moment of recognition, a moment that was solitary moments removed from the happy and loving words that this careful woman had written in moments closer to her childhood than to the present. Affectionate and sweet, positive and loving, her words presented evidence that something indeed had existed between us, a force that had made us believers in love, something that had given us the hope to bring children into the world, believing that being together was a lifelong possibility.

I knew that I had felt similar emotions for her, before we started living our separate lives under the same roof. Now, my heart was disquieted and made uneasy, akin to nauseated, when I read these sweet words, realizing that at one time she found me to be lovable and lovely. It had been so long since the nectar of affection had dripped from her pen or her tongue that I had ceased to believe that I had ever tasted it.

I'd walked down this riverbed many times in the five years since our parting; it had hardened many years before, nothing grew, nothing remained, and it was hard to imagine that the flimsy vessel called "Us" had ever scraped its keel along the shallow waterway to nowhere.

Now I had stubbed my toe on a fossil.

At some unremembered moment, that box of letters had been put away, buried and forgotten, no more letters came, and syrup no longer flowed up from the cold New England ground, no longer circled round the rings of a sturdy maple, and no longer gushed into a wooden bucket with my name on it. Back then, I wondered what was wrong with me, accepting that I was unattractive to her, but not fully knowing why.

Now, nearly five years divorced, I wondered these things again. Had we both changed, or had we both revealed our true selves? I couldn't say; perhaps a combination of the two. My one certainty was that her garage held an even larger box, with many, many more pledges of my once undying love. I always was the wordy one.

I started skimming then tossing her letters into the large trash bin outside the open garage door. An unsettling feeling overcame me. I felt as if I were involved in some unsavory endeavor, betrayal, theft, murder, cover-up, or other crime. Had I read her words, loving and happy, endearing in their innocence and faith in love, only to discard them?

I finally arrested myself, and pulled every last letter out of the trash bin. I thought of calling E and asking if she wanted the letters, but didn't know if it would seem like an insult to say that I was ridding myself of these words. So, I called my daughters and asked them if they wanted them. Yes was the resounding answer, so I wrapped them with a rubber band and gave them to the girls the next time they came over.

Finding those letters was odd and sad, disturbing and yet reassuring. On the one hand, it was nice to know that at some time in our romance and marriage, E declared love for me, but on the other, that magnified the fact that at some point we had lost something. What was it? What had changed about either or both of us?

I am thinking about love. I am wondering about the man I am in this moment, a man reborn who loves a woman, a man discovering something in my heart that I have never given to anyone until now, either because it was not there to give, or because I had no idea how to give it.

Yes, that giant box that sits in E's garage is full of pledges and puppy love, written by a boy who didn't have a clue about carrying out the task of love. I only knew how to spell.

Weeks before we married, I told my father that I wanted to make sure the wedding vows he was to lead us through contained all the right biblical elements of a wedding. Damn, I was so full of information, fresh out of the Love Inn cult, having learned nothing. I wanted to be the head of the house, and wanted to be submitted to as such.

Dad looked at me like I was insane.

He opened his Bible and read the full passage I was gleaning from, in which a husband's love is so great for his wife, he'll lay down his life for her. His point was well taken — scripture calls men to sacrifice, not bullishness. He gently corrected my eagerness to have a "godly marriage," and brought some sense of humility to me before the ring was on E's finger.

I knew nothing in those days. I wasn't watching closely enough.

I am reaching, reaching, stretching far back, trying to glimpse my father, the most loving person I can remember. I want to watch him keeping the flame of love stoked and burning, and as he comes into focus, I see not the tokens of romance, the words and music of well-orchestrated gestures, lavish gifts, and not even the muscle-straining work of breadwinning.

No, his fire is contained and steady. His arms around my mother calm her and give her confidence. He wields not a gavel or a scepter, but a mop, and he bids her to rest a while as he washes the kitchen floor, rendering the footprints of their dance visible only to their private remembrance.

And so I imitate him, and summon his spirit to find that place in my soul that is ready to love like a grownup, and in doing so, I ask my Southern Born Woman where she keeps her bucket and mop.

23

Snow Angels

Snow rarely falls in Nashville. Every seven or eight years, we get hit with a modest yet incapacitating bit of weather, maybe four inches of fluff.

These days, technology sees it coming, and a day or two before the winter storm blows in, grocery stores are filled with those who know just how crippling a few inches of snow can be in our town. There is a collective bracing of ourselves, as we wonder how many days of school will be canceled, and how long will it take for the sun to clear our roads, as there is reportedly only one snowplow in our fair city. Faucets are set to drip, so that pipes don't freeze. Whether you own a cat or not, a few fifty-pound bags of kitty litter are placed in the trunk of your car, for traction.

Winter in Nashville is complicated.

On one snowy Friday evening, my Dearest Companion and I were having a glass of Bushmill's when I got an emergency call from my nephew Dave, who told me that my good friend of three decades, Tom Howard, had died moments before.

Tom, a Minnesota native, had been walking in the snow with his wife and some friends, when he fell back, and dropped dead. One of the friends told me it was the most horrible thing she'd ever witnessed—a man down, his wife begging him not to leave her, and helpless friends standing by as the snow quietly covered any sign that they'd been there.

Tom and I met in Upstate New York in the late 70s, when he was a "Jesus Music" recording artist. We immediately had a rapport, two funny guys riffing off each other like Dizzy Gillespie and Charlie Parker. His personality was a mix: brooding genius, swarthy gentleman, extroverted absurdist, and stressed-out milquetoast. Over the years, we'd run into each other at various concerts or events, until we finally became neighbors in Nashville.

We became Wednesday evening regulars at the same pub, the Sherlock Holmes, where Guinness was on tap before it became a household word. Our Wednesday gathering was usually quite large, requiring several ample tables, tended to by one barmaid, whose name was Moira. Moira was the widow of Nicky Hopkins, the famous session player, whose piano work graced recordings of the Rolling Stones, the Who, the Beatles, and a host of British Invasion rock groups.

Wednesday night drinking at Sherlock's was as much a given for me as Wednesday night prayer meeting had been for my Baptist father. Smoke rings, darts, and fish and chips were nearly sacramental, and as a night wore on, and inhibitions wore down, our little congregation lifted jokes, arguments, discussions, and diatribes with the fervor of backslidden Pentecostals.

One night, Bob Saporiti, then a VP at Warner Brothers Records, started passing a guitar around. Bob wasn't a part of our group, but on this particular evening, his guitar floated from table to table, where anyone who was willing could sing a song.

It was an opportunity of sorts. In a room full of songwriters, here was your chance to get the ear of a Nashville power broker. For once, the expensive pints might prove to be a sound investment, if only Bob Saporiti handed you his card, saying, "Give me a call tomorrow when you've sobered up"; perhaps it would lead to something.

The guitar finally came to Tom, a musician of considerable talent.

Tom waited for the room to quiet down and started playing "Blowing in the Wind" in G. With an angelic expression on his face, Tom sincerely looked each of us in the eye, and then he did something that is nearly impossible for even a good musician to do.

He began to sing in G sharp.

Most of the room buckled over in laughter, as he maintained the simultaneous, clashing keys with a completely straight face, earnestly singing Bob Dylan's most famous song. A few drinkers were miffed and upset, as if Tom were dousing Dylan's sheet music in urine, but he sang the entire song without cracking a smile.

When he was done, Saporiti took his guitar back.

That was the last time anyone ever passed a guitar around Sherlock's.

One of Tom's greatest gifts was laughing at himself. There was a klutz-proneness about Tom, an extraordinary ability to spill wine on your carpet, set fire to your shirt, and put a hole in your guitar...all in the same evening.

He would regale friends with outrageous tales of his faux pas, like the time he slipped and accidentally bloodied the lip of a woman hosting a dinner party, or how he feigned spraying beer all over the same party's guests, and then realized the bottle wasn't empty after it was too late.

By making himself so very vulnerable to people, Tom had collected a lot of friends. He was generous to anyone who knew him, offering a hand, encouragement, and goodwill to everyone he encountered.

Once, I told him that I had never used my garage as shelter for my car. I explained that there was too much junk in it. He offered to help me clear out the mess, so we rented a pickup truck one day and got the job done. As we worked, our conversation digressed from life's crises to theology to gossip to humor.

Another trait of Tom's was to believe for the best until the very end. When marriages were on the rocks, he would proclaim, "They'll be back together." Sometimes he was right. He had a gift of faith. I remember protesting to him, "But she's so much better off without him!" Tom just wanted things to work out for everyone.

Being in an industry that works like a poorly maintained roller coaster, Tom often encouraged me in my career, saying year after year, "This year's gonna be your year!" When I had victories, he would smile and say, "I told you so," smiling like an older brother.

Once, I was hired to play at a gala honoring Emmylou Harris. At the rehearsal, I had trouble with the piano intro to "Sweet Dreams," which Elvis Costello was to perform. Elvis wanted me to play it like the great Steve Nieve had played it on their 1981 recording. I'll never forget sitting at my keyboard during the rehearsal, with Elvis standing over me, watching me fumble my way through the song. The brutal reality that I was *not* Steve Nieve led to my dialing Tom late in the evening the night before the show.

"I'm out of my league, and I need to practice on a real piano. Can I come over?"

Tom opened his door to me at about 11:00 p.m. and let me sit at his beautiful grand piano for the next hour until I had assimilated Nieve's intro. Tom had a natural gift for encouragement. A couple of years later, I was asked to join Emmylou's band, and who knows what might have happened if I had botched the intro to "Sweet Dreams," a song she has been identified with for years.

Often Tom would remind friends, "I'm praying for you."

Cut to the snowy evening in Nashville.

My nephew's words, "Tom is dead," brought light tears to my eyes, and yet a smile to my lips. I knew Tom. Tom was one of the few people in my life who could leave his friends behind with little doubt of how he felt toward them. Maybe it was time to be riffing with his Maker.

I called my kids and told them Tom was gone. Then I turned my phone off.

The snow bogged Nashville down for about four days. No one was going anywhere.

When Sunday evening came, my car was stuck a few streets from the site of Tom's wake, so I donned my boots and trudged across crunching snow and skidded on black ice until I found myself standing in Ben Pearson's kitchen with a glass of cabernet.

I looked around the room. I saw old friends like fellow bluesman Dave Perkins and painter Dorsey McHugh, whose name alone could make her lovable. Jimmy Abegg, my longtime friend and fellow traveler, embraced me and kissed my cheek.

I was caught off-guard by a friend with whom I had fallen out of favor. He extended his hand, which I shook briefly, and then let go of. Tom's ability to accept his friends' foibles was highlighted in this moment of awkwardness with two people who had come to some sort of silent agreement to let go of friendship. I think Tom would have loved the idea of his wake bringing two people back together, such was the level of his optimism and hope in relationships.

In this case, that didn't happen. But if Tom were reading this, he'd be saying, "Give it time."

Regardless of our differences, we were all there for the same reason; we loved this great man who had been taken by stress or a bad heart, or by an impatient God Almighty. Like God Almighty, Tom loved everyone in that room.

Like the snow that covered Tom's last footprints, the gift of his love was able to cover a multitude of weaknesses, burying the staggered footprints that our errant feet had tracked through each other's lives.

Eventually, I approached Tom's widow and embraced her. She whispered assuring words of comfort to me, and then cracked a joke. "She's in the Mercy Time," my Dearest Companion later remarked, noting how often the bereaved will find themselves in the role of comforting the less bereaved.

When someone whistled for silence, people moved toward the

whistle. I backed away from it. I hoped that the evening would stay intimate, and that there would be no speechmaking. Not long ago, I would have been an enthusiastic participant at such an event. Now, I just wanted to quietly remember him without the grandstanding.

Plastic cups of wine were raised for a moment, and people went back to the conversations they had been having. I was glad that the moment hadn't snowballed into a round robin of oration, feeling that the quiet reminiscences were purer and more trustworthy than the performances speeches would likely turn into.

I finally put on my overcoat and gloves and headed for the door. I thought about the wide landscape of Tom's friendships as I left, warmed by Dave's smile, Dorsey's affectionate remembrances, and Jimmy's reminder that he and I were "friends before we ever met."

As I walked past Belmont Baptist Church, the moon shone bright and full, illuminating my snowy path with blue light, emphasizing the melancholy that hummed behind my eyes.

My ears reddened in the frozen air, and I picked up my pace. I listened to my racing heart and I thought about Tom's approaching funeral. I wondered if it would bring closure to those of us who missed him. I hoped it would be about Tom, not about those who loved him. I thought about funerals past, particularly my dad's, which seemed hijacked by good intentions and abject neediness. I knew that truly saying good-bye to Tom meant finding a quiet place, even quieter than the moonlit path that lay before me.

As I walked, it occurred to me that we can never really say good-bye to those who die before we do, and that the silence we seek is found only in the presence that embraces the departed, with snow-white wings.

24

The Long Ride Home

They strolled down the midway, bored, it seemed to me. Their fists wrapped around stalks of cotton candy and enormous cups of Pepsi, as they took in as much excess as an amusement park could offer. Sooner or later, their buckling legs and aching feet brought them to the bandstand where a Christian music concert was happening. This was a nearly captive audience, sleeveless, sunburned, and red-necked. Weary of thrill seeking, they were ours for a song or two, and then they'd leave to see if the line for the roller coaster had gotten any shorter.

This was sometime around 1991. I was in Nowhere, Kentucky, playing Hammond organ, backing a gospel singer, and trying to look engaged with the music. I was filling in for the regular keyboardist, and while I played the right notes, I was aware that I was more of an onlooker than a participant in what felt like a carnival sideshow.

In the performance arts, there are times when you know that something *real* is happening, and other times when you wonder if it's just an act. The singer waved a handkerchief, fanning some imaginary flame, as if to imply that something extraordinary was occurring on the heels of his golden voice. The music seemed secondary to the snake-oil antics, which were hell-bent on whipping the crowd into a frenzy. I have never been able to go whole hog for anything like

Pentecostalism, yet here I was, cranking away on a Hammond organ, spinning the Leslie speaker as if it were a dizzying ride on the Tilt-A-Whirl, just like Old Scratch on his calliope.

A few die-hard fans in the audience were enrapt, as if God Almighty was a mischievous puppeteer, stirring them to shouting and lifting their hands in the air, their bodies jerking out of time with the music. I wondered if the Holy Ghost were impersonating Ralph Kramden. Bang! Zoom! The band was all smiles, and to the crowd, it probably looked like the joy of the Lord on their faces, but to me it looked like they were all in on the same joke. I considered the possibility that everyone in the band was experiencing an epiphany except for me. Wouldn't have been the first time. Maybe that was the joke I wasn't connecting with.

Back in the green room, I had run into a singer we were sharing the bill with, Kathy Troccoli. She and I were old friends, and in the process of catching up, she told me that her mother had recently died. She said that her mother's passing was beautiful, grateful that she had been present when the moment of departure had come.

After the show was over, we disembarked for Nashville. As soon as we left the park, our tour bus died. We wound up renting a car and heading back to Nashville. No one spoke as we wound our way South, each of us caught up in private silence.

As we rode down the interstate, I pictured Kathy by her mother's deathbed, an image that soon morphed into a series of pictures of whoever came to mind. My thoughts found themselves in California at the bedside of a friend who was in the hospital, having had a heart attack. I didn't know that he was soon to have a second, fatal attack, and yet my thoughts of him sank in the fathomless reality that life is short.

My musings turned to my father, who hadn't yet been overcome with Alzheimer's, and was to be with us for another fifteen years. I tried to imagine the feeling of being with him as he passed into Glory Land. Why I became transfixed by this idea, I can't say, but in the silence of a conversationless car, I wrapped myself in a comforter of melancholy and thought about this man I feared losing.

Morbid thoughts cascaded into a snowdrift of poetry, and I began playing a memory game with myself, silently repeating new lines and the ones that preceded them. By the time I got to Nashville, I had a sad, yet hopeful song called "Goodbye for the Last Time."

The song was the first of many I would write about grieving, loss, dying, and crossing over. I went to one of the Christian record companies and proposed a concept record about loss and grieving, an idea that was well received. After all, if anyone would be open to a discussion about death and dying, I assumed it would be Christians, for whom the Resurrection says "O Death, where is thy sting?"

Meetings ensued in which executives and I brainstormed over sushi, reviewing songs and dreaming about the big-name artists who would perform these pieces. Somewhere along the journey, my idea was confiscated and turned into something a little less taboo, a little less dark, and I found myself with a hat full of tunes that might never find a home.

The gatekeepers of Christian culture (for lack of a better word) don't know how to talk about dying. Like Albert King sang, "Everybody wants to go to Heaven, but nobody wants to die."

I retreated from my notion of making meaningful music for the Christian market.

In the meantime, Dad's Alzheimer's became more pronounced and instead of fearing his death, I began hoping for it.

Years after his memory had departed, my father passed on, and had I been there to hold his hand, he wouldn't have known it until, perhaps, a millisecond between this world and the next.

This is how I found out that Dad was gone:

I woke up early on November 29, 2006, to take my daughters, Kate and Maddy, to school. My virtual stack of emails included one from my mother to just about everyone in the world, which announced the death of my father. A few minutes later, my phone rang, and I heard Annie's shaking voice calling from Ireland to tell me what cyberspace had already broadcast. I said, "I already know. I just got an email from Mom to about a thousand people."

I had spent my childhood sharing my father with his parishioners, and now I was no more important than any of them in the hierarchy of finding out about his death. My mother made funeral arrangements that seemed to have more consideration of his old flock than his own children. We buried him a month after he died, to insure that all of his former congregants would be able to make plans to attend.

I made mental notes about what not to do when I died.

As is often the case, I turned my musings into songs. I reconsidered recording music to accompany the grief process.

I called a friend at Alive Hospice in Nashville, who might have a perspective on death and dying that hadn't occurred to me. We met one Friday morning at the Alive Hospice campus, a bright and cheerful set of buildings near Music Row.

After talking for a while, Pam offered me the "nickel tour" of the facility, and I accepted. I wasn't sure what to expect, but I assumed I would encounter somber sights, sounds, and smells similar to those of the nursing home Mormor, my maternal grandmother, had lived her final days in.

Such was not the case.

Every effort had been made to make the live-in facility as un-cliniclike as possible. Pam showed me a vacant dorm room, which had little furniture in it, explaining that patients often like to have a favorite chair or dresser brought from home. Similarly, the walls are bare because many people like to hang their favorite pictures around their room.

The social workers who work at Alive Hospice encourage patients to be honest about their needs, and try to see that even the wildest of wishes might be fulfilled for a patient in his or her last days. One patient, a camping enthusiast, wanted to spend a night camping with her best friend. A tent was set up in the courtyard area, and her wish was fulfilled.

Walking down a corridor filled with original art, Pam explained that one of the residential patients was an artist who wanted to show her work. The staff hung her paintings and invited her friends and family to her art show, and gave her a true sense of having meaning and something to live for right to the end.

When I had seen all there was to see, Pam and I shook hands and said good-bye. As I left, I began thinking about this journey we're all on. A journey that I believe leads to somewhere and Someone.

I thought about how well my mother took care of Dad during his long bout with Alzheimer's, and how she enjoyed being with him even when it was unclear whether he understood who she was.

I thought about the friends I've lost over the last decade to illness or accidents—Tom, Jackie, Janice, and Mark. And I thought of friends who'd survived calamity and illness—Ralston, Buddy, Dave, and John Arthur.

I thought of my Dearest Companion.

And it occurred to me, driving away from Alive Hospice, that life affords everyone the ironic opportunity to accompany those we love on the long ride to Somewhere. We don't often think this way unless something catastrophic happens, but in truth, loving someone is all about making that person comfortable en route to the next life.

What if today was my Southern Born Woman's last? How would I be any different? Maybe I would speak a little softer, listen a little harder, smile a little wider, and pull her a little closer.

I can play all the right notes, but what does it matter if I'm not engaged in the music of living? I'm thinking of that day backstage at the amusement park, when a friend's story of bereavement gave me a song, and when the gospel group entertained whoever had ears to hear. Maybe I was wrong about them. Maybe they were caught up in the joy of knowing exactly what they were doing, and perhaps the joke they were in on was that they were serenading people who were getting ready for the long ride home.

25

The Chick Upstairs

God knows she's a mystery. She plays like a song in my head that I can't turn off, because I'm still wrapping my mind around its meaning and its structure. She's a complex blues tune, beyond three chords and the truth. She's a melody that rolls like "Georgia On My Mind" or "Send Me Someone to Love." And her lyric, well, don't ask me. Maybe she taught Dylan his stuff, and William Blake, too.

She defines passion. She's got a temper, fiery and hot, but not before her graceful patience is pushed to the edge of reason. Occasionally, regret drives her to extremes, but the immensity of her heart somehow reins in her contradictions; try as I might, I can't find fault with her.

And Lord, she's got a killer sense of humor.

She's as understanding as only a mother can be. Sometimes I imagine her asking, "Philip, where did you come from anyway?" as my own mother used to ask when baffled by her bluesman son's antics. But this woman knows the path of my pilgrimage better than anyone, because she has walked every mile of it, occasionally leading the way, more likely warily tagging along. She appreciates when I stop and ask for directions, but knows that more often than not, I'll go all male on her and seek to find my destination without help.

She's all-loving, but never doting. Omnipresent, but not annoyingly so. She'll give you all the space you want.

And, Lord, she's handy, like a good shade-tree mechanic. She'll repair that aching engine of mine every so often, cooling it down just by laying her hand on my heart.

God Almighty. The Chick Upstairs.

In truth, I call Her "Him" because my picture of God is decidedly paternal. Growing up with a reasonable and loving dad never made the masculine image of God anything but good to my eyes. My mother and her mother before her wouldn't have engendered my trust for a feminized she-god, meddlesome and insistent upon always being right. Oh, Lord, She'd be bugging me about washing my hands, and reading my Bible, and changing my underwear just in case I wind up in the emergency room. I wouldn't be able to question Her without being accused of blasphemy.

I imagine God the Father quietly nodding as I ramble on, giving me a grin like my old man would have when I played some boogie-woogie version of a hymn, and kissing me on the lips when I showed unannounced at his back door.

Nonetheless, I'm not sure what's so riling when some Christians encounter inclusive language regarding the Person of God. I still cross myself and the brows of my woman and my children, intoning the words "Father, Son, and Holy Spirit," and am quite comfortable doing so. At Christ Church Cathedral, the traditional language of the Trinity is sometimes altered to "Creator, Savior, and Sanctifier." I recently read of a proposal in the Presbyterian Church to use this alteration: "Mother, Child, and Womb." What can I say? Point well taken, but…*womb*? I'll take the comfort, but not the claustrophobia. What happens when *that* line gets translated back to male language?

The Gospel narrative is beautiful to me with its perfectly loving parent, sending the willing heir to save a reckless world from itself. The language of love is hard to put into words; in our attempt to pull the Divine down to our level, we forget that God has already descended to us in Christ, coming as a servant. In Divine Servitude, perhaps God allows for our tainted images of Him/Her/It, if only to begin an eternal conversation. And perhaps our blurred images diffuse the blinding beam of Who God is, so that we can endure the light of God's presence.

While I don't have a particular need to see God as She, I find it amusing that believers want to limit the scope of God's image to "The Man Upstairs."

We like to see God as one of our type.

God Almighty, maker of Heaven and earth, existed before gender, before limitations. And a great irony of the Creation, in whatever manner it occurred, is that things came into focus and definition, and Humankind gave those things names, from Armadillos to Zebras.

When God's glory was exhibited to those nomadic Hebrews of old, they would proclaim him "Lion of Judah," "Morning Star," or "Rock of my salvation," giving definition and understanding to an infinite and fathomless God. Someone somewhere has probably likened God unto an armadillo. If we can call God "Rock," "Lion," "Star," why not "Mother"?

There are those who want to keep the masculinity of God intact, and there are those who want to neuter Him completely. Neither party seems to be in it for the praise of God but more likely for the praise of its own identity. Even so, it's as if an involuntary muscle is acquiescing to the notion of God Incarnate, God among us, Emmanuel. Or should I say Emmanuelle?

Growing up in my father's fairly progressive Baptist Church, it was only a matter of time before I encountered a real live Christian feminist. Sue possessed a forceful presence. Her passion was the reclamation of a woman's full measure of self and place. She and her husband would often have me over for a meal, and inevitably, conversation would turn toward Dad's church and how not enough was happening to advance women in our congregation.

Sue would criticize a prayer that Dad had intoned, wishing it had been more inclusive, and bemoaning the word "Father," which Dad often used in addressing God. Naturally, I was defensive of my dad, knowing his heart, and particularly knowing how often he had made strides for the advancement of women within his church governing body. It was Dad, with great encouragement from my mother, who made sure women could serve Communion and become deacons at Barrington Baptist. Sue must have known this, because she continued to attend.

Years later, when I was an elder in a conservative Presbyterian (PCA) church for a brief season, I cringed at the fact that PCA women were relegated to bake sales and nursery duty, and barred from leadership roles. Thus, when we elders would convene to nominate new elders and deacons, the names I threw in the hat were those of capable women. My fellow elders chuckled at my apparent lack of theological correctness, and nothing changed. At least Sue would have been proud of me for trying.

When a friend sent me a book called *The Shack*, I was intrigued by the author's device of using a large, black woman to portray the parental image of God. Yet, the Almighty Matron was called "Papa" in the book, perhaps giving a full acknowledgment that God was at once male and female.

The male and female facets of God's self have been distributed to humankind in ways that are manageable and portable in this lifetime. Perhaps, when the Almighty gathers us all together in that great day of Christ's return, we will be restored to a likeness of God that is equally full of the feminine and the masculine.

We cling to what we know, good and bad. God can reveal Himself in beautiful, redemptive movements yet remain stigmatized by the images we confine Him to. If being someone's child was a less than wonderful experience, it's likely that we'll imagine God the Father or Mother as a killjoy who douses our passions with the glib fact of His lack of interest in us.

So, one turns away from the blurry image of a Curmudgeon God, and picks up a paintbrush and allows a canvas to dictate an unforeseeable outcome. And as if from dust, something of beauty appears, something of our own making. This is why we write, paint, compose, and imagine, and that is the only kind of predestination that makes sense to me: We were created to imitate our Creator.

Created in God's image, we create. When it comes to theology, we tend to create God in our own image.

In our search for intimacy with the Divine, given to imagination as we are, we give our image of God a shape and an identity that we can put our trust in. The idea of a shape-shifting God is beautiful; this is a confident God, adaptable and congenial in His willingness to be seen from another angle, yet with His character remaining fully intact. The triune God revealed as Creator, Savior, and Sanctifier, unbound by our imagination, yet bound to the integrity of who only God Almighty can be. God.

It's hard for me to see Christ as something other than God the Son, but it's not difficult to embrace the Oneness of the Trinity as gender-free and shapeless, magnificent in Its mystery, confident in Its mission to reconcile the world unto Itself, and earnestly being about the creative business of redemption.

So much of my own redemption has come in the form of the woman who loves me that considering God Almighty as feminine seems plausible and attractive to me, not that God will be emasculated, but that His vastness will be made larger to me.

He, She, It. Ai ai ai. Sometimes the better names might be what God Almighty is doing: Redemption. Restoration. Rejuvenation. Revelation.

Beholding the burning bush, Moses asked God Almighty for some identification, and heard the words "I am."

In a way, that's all that matters. The Chick Upstairs simply *is*.

26

Faith and the Details

On New Year's Eve 2009, my Dearest Companion had carved out some private time for herself and her beautiful daughters, something of a parenthesis in our evening, or perhaps it was I who was the parentheses in *their* evening. Having two of my own daughters, I understand the sacred space of Girlworld, and thus found myself with time to kill before Old Man Time introduced the new decade.

I decided to head over to my friend Alayna's, where a particularly lavish bash was simmering. My friends Asher and Missy introduced me to a young man named Mat.

"Phil, do you know Mat Kearney?"

I had heard of Mat, a successful recording artist, but had never met him nor had I heard his music.

The next thing I knew, I was recruiting him to be a part of my non-gospel Gospel project, *Mercyland: Hymns For The Rest Of Us*. Of course, this was months before I had a title, but Mat liked the concept of an inclusive record of new spirituals.

We met for breakfast at Bongo Java, a Nashville hot spot, and talked about the project. We discussed my recurring theme of wanting to send a positive message about God, to offset the frowning icon that much of Christendom has hung outside its impenetrable walls.

We retreated to his car, which was reassuringly messy; I felt right at home as we listened to the artists I'd already recorded for the project: Emmylou Harris, The Civil Wars, and yours truly.

Mat was game.

A few weeks later, we met at the Bombay Bistro for a curry. Enjoying the medium burn of some spicy Chicken Tikka Massala, we talked about life and love. Mat was making wedding plans, bright-eyed and confident. I spoke candidly, as is my way, trying not to imply that I, a divorced man, embodied his future, and yet knowing that I represent half of all marriages: failed.

His joyous beginning juxtaposed with my sobering story was a metaphor for the way life is. Our conversation was heavy and light, funny and sad, sad and funny. We were both laughing by the time lunch ended. Life is what it is.

We finally headed back to my studio, picked up our guitars, and started exploring. Mat's old mahogany Martin sounded beautiful, and as he played he sang whatever syllables seemed right. This beautiful, nonsensical singing reminded me of Love Inn, where people would erupt in melodic songs of ecstatic utterances, "tongues," they called it. Could've been. Whatever it was, it seemed earnest enough.

But when Mat's broken words flew, they were circling an idea, and eventually a song with real words began taking shape. No interpretation needed.

A story started appearing, a story told in the first person, of a wounded man who is blessed with a child, then wounded by the cycle of her life, and finally left bereft, all the while wondering how God is found in the details, a question whose impossible answers lead to more questions.

The writing of a song is sometimes a mystical experience, depending on one's methods and one's goals, and depending upon the chemistry between the writers. An openness to the Muse means unchaining one's consciousness from an agenda, and a willingness to ride the wind. Sometimes, the song writes itself, and when a listener later declares the writer "brilliant," the honest composer will know that something happened quite outside him- or herself.

Often, a writer's casually tossed phrase is snagged like a prize tuna by his or her cowriter, and a song is born. More often, writers sit in silence waiting for the idea to surface. And when one writes alone, it's my experience that personal drama, joy, pain, or circumstance must accompany the endeavor for one to achieve anything of substance.

Mat and I threw ideas back and forth, challenged each other's thinking, pondered silently, cutting and pasting, and rearranging letters as if playing Scrabble, until we had our song, "Walking Over the Water." A few months later, we recorded it in a small studio outside Nashville.

The question of God in the details will continue to haunt me. I thank God for my daily bread, while wondering if I've been chosen to be taken care of while some earthquake-ruined Haitian has been forsaken.

The ocean of life is happening all around us, joy, love, happiness, prosperity, victory, yet not excluding death, loss, failure, sadness. It's hard to be thankful on the downside of the wave.

I'm not sure what to do with all my questions. Steve Earle is right. *I'm not God.*

Perhaps my constant questioning is yet another way to praise, not much different from the splashing sound of melodic tongues over a fathomless ocean of wonder, as if the nagging is yet another affirmation, proof, and exclamation circling the throne of God Almighty like countless singing Cherubim.

27

Water

Easter is the Big One when it comes to holy days.

I like Christmas better than Easter, because I'm sentimental. I like watching *It's A Wonderful Life* and *A Christmas Story*, and between those two films, I have a substantial hook on which to hang my stocking cap full of sentimentality.

Not to mention Jesus being born so humbly and quietly in the back slums of Bethlehem, under a lone star, never mind his miraculous conception or his sweet young parents.

And then there's the music, both sacred and secular, from "Joy to the World" to "The Christmas Song"; I can sit down and play just about any secular Christmas standard from memory, ad nauseam. Perhaps I'm subconsciously celebrating the Incarnation when I start plunking out "I'll Be Home for Christmas."

Christmas gives us memories that are carried forward for years. Heart-warming or blood-chilling, Christmas leaves a memory or a mark.

Yet Easter, the celebration of Christ's resurrection, is what really matters most to Christianity. There's nothing sentimental about the death, burial, and resurrection of Jesus. It's not warm and fuzzy like the cotton cloth you want to wrap the Baby Jesus in. Holy Week is more of a spiritual emotional journey—Hope welcomed and celebrated, Hope betrayed, Hope put to death, and Hope coming back to life in victory. Nothing sappy about that.

Easter is a holy day, not a holiday. No one fondly recalls a particular childhood Easter, but more likely will lump the egg hunts and Easter baskets of the past into one collective Easter memory.

I can't remember any Easters before Easter 2008. I remember '08 because it wasn't all that long ago, and because the newness of love was in my life. I picked up my Southern Born Woman in the earlyish hours and went to Christ Cathedral. I don't remember anything of the service, nor about the lunch I'm certain we shared afterward. Neither of us was in a particularly resurrected mood, and the weather was gray, but I remember that I was with her, and glad of it.

Easter 2009 was a good one. My Dearest Companion went with one of her daughters to an early sunrise service put on for homeless Nashvillians; they were eager to hear Del Rio, a homeless preacher who'd spoken in years past. They liked the sound of his name, and they repeated it soulfully, as if the name "Del Rio" tasted like barbecue in Memphis, rolling the spicy syllables around in their mouths.

Much to their disappointment, Del Rio didn't show. A seminary student spoke, lofty and intelligent, perhaps condescending, and certainly without the soul of Del Rio, thus disappointing the two Southern Born Women. Following the sunrise service, they met me at the cathedral, where, trust me, nothing tastes like Memphis.

The sanctuary was packed with Belle Meade socialites dressed to the nines, a few homeless folks, regulars, and irregulars. The bishop delivered a fine sermon; the choir was accompanied by a brass section, and my memory was vaguely stirred with the singing of "Christ the Lord Is Risen Today," Easter's most popular hymn.

We skipped out before the benediction and dropped the younger SBW at her father's church, which sits prominently above a buzzing Nashville neighborhood called Green Hills. Ninety minutes later, we had read the *New York Times* and shared a pot of Lady Grey tea, and headed back up the hill to retrieve said daughter, upon which we encountered her father and his new girlfriend, as if to highlight the new season that Easter represents.

Finally, we got to the only thing that mattered anymore on this fine Easter Sunday—the restaurant where we had made brunch reservations. My daughters arrived, along with their cousin Dave and his wife, Liz, and my brother David and his wife, Lynda, who were visiting from Washington State.

Sitting there with David, I realized that although we don't look much alike, we share traits our father passed on to us. For example, we both get misty-eyed when we speak of sentimental or holy things. My brother relayed the theme of a sermon he'd recently heard, one in which the blues were exalted, along with gospel music, and the idea that a life well-lived can't have one without the other. It was an idea that resonated with all of us, and as he told it, I thought, *He's got tears in his eyes, runs in the family.*

This wasn't a new discovery to me, but a recognition that he's always done this, and so have I, but when did *always* begin? Were we this way before divorce and failure made, I hope, more merciful men out of us? The more I think about this, the more I come to believe that it's more a function of genetics than anything else, because Dad was the same way, and he hadn't been broken by divorce or failure; he'd lived a wonderfully successful life when it comes to marriage and family, and just plain living.

I was a child when I first took note of Dad's easy tears. We were at the movies together, watching the end of *Old Yeller*, when I realized that even grown men could cry.

I wish my eyes didn't tear up when I'm moved. I find this trait an inconvenience, a distraction, and a betrayal of sentimentality.

I wonder if Dad, too, was annoyed by his propensity to moistened eyes when he felt the weightlessness of being loved.

Since my father apparently bequeathed his misty eyes to me, I accept the gift as something intrinsically wonderful, because he certainly was.

I grasp for anything that might put me in Dad's league. So much of my behavior pulls me away from the kind of man he was, a pure, unvulgar, beautiful human being with an amazing capacity for tolerance and understanding. I know he loved Mom like no one else, and he loved his children in such a way that we each thought we were his favorite child. And, despite my broken, overstated earthiness, I *do* know how to love. And I got that from him.

When Dad died in 2006, I choked up, but didn't weep. His Alzheimer's had taken him from us long before his heart had stopped beating, and I felt that I had already grieved for him in those preceding years of loss. I thought that it was fitting for him to depart so close to Thanksgiving, as I was truly thankful that his suffering was done with.

There was a month-long gap between his death and his funeral, giving me plenty of time to collect myself before eulogizing him.

On Christmas Day, my daughters and I, along with their mother, boarded a plane and flew to Providence for the service. E and the girls stayed with her stepmother, while I bunked in at the Providence Radisson with Rob Grant, a close friend for most of my life.

My brother, David, and I each had written eulogies, which we had kept to ourselves. We knew we would far exceed the three minutes we were each allotted to give tribute, but neither of us was going to send Dad off without fully celebrating him.

I was confident that I would ascend the steps to the pulpit and deliver my remembrance of Dad with a dry eye. Within the first ten seconds, my voice was quivering, and I knew I was in for a difficult ride. However, as the Funny Guy, I was able to laugh through my tears, and tell the packed house about the lovely human being we now celebrated.

Once, I said, I had visited Dad and Mom at their assisted-living facility near Hartford, and Dad looked at me with an expression of familiarity. At first I thought, *He knows me.* Then I realized, *He probably thinks he's looking in the mirror.* Those who remembered him saw the uncanny resemblance.

I spoke of Dad's love of the New York Yankees, a brave position to take in the heart of Red Sox country; I reflected on Dad buying David and me Yankee jackets and hats. In a quiet gesture, Dad had marked his sons as distinctly his. I remarked that it was only out of respect for Dad's grieving widow, a lifelong Red Sox fan, that I hadn't donned a Yankee cap for his sendoff into what must certainly be eternal Yankee Territory.

I recalled a man in the congregation having told me that Dad was the first man who ever hugged him. That simple fact was the distillation of who my father really was, a person whose main business was loving people. If anyone was a natural at his job, Dad was.

I confessed that I couldn't remember whether Dad was a great preacher, although I knew I'd been a living, breathing anthology of illustrations for his sermons, particularly highlighting Humankind's fallen nature. Where he was a great preacher, however, was in the living of his life, a man given to kindness and mercy.

More than anyone I've ever met, my dad exemplified unconditional love. Believers and nonbelievers alike were welcome in his world. I used to marvel how Dad knew the names of so many people who were not connected to church. He was genuinely friendly to everyone.

Finally, I said that he may have forgotten the names of his children long before he passed, but even at the end, he'd been running on the fumes of God Almighty. Not long before he died, Dad still had the ability to sing a hymn. Once, my mother discovered him sitting with his Bible, trying to read it, not realizing that it was upside-down. Enough memory remained that he knew that there was something special about this leather-bound book, even if the concept of reading was lost on him. Scripture was so woven into the fabric of his heart that it was one of the last things to go. His love of God was so ingrained that even Alzheimer's had a difficult time expunging the evidence that he was a genuine man of love.

As I spoke, my eyes weren't misty; they were flooded. I wept under the weight of loss, with the recognition that no matter how much I believe in the Resurrection, one day without Dad in this world may as well be eternity. I wept for a world bereft of this vessel of goodness and decency, and wondered how Heaven could possibly need Dad any more than this old world needed him.

I wept as a man who looks every bit his father's son, but knows how fully his heart must be resurrected in order for the imitation to become real.

I am mindful of the notion that God Almighty keeps a bottle in which nothing evaporates; in which precious ointment, perfume, or oil may as well be treasured.

Lo, it's filled with tears.

28

Passion Fruits

Nearly every October of the new millennium, I have traveled to San Francisco to participate in a free music festival called Hardly Strictly Bluegrass, given to the city by financier Warren Hellman.

In 2009, I had two Hardly Strictly appearances to make, one with Buddy Miller, whose band I had been a part of for many years, and the other with Emmylou Harris. Having plenty of time to enjoy this beautiful city, my Southern Born Woman joined me for a relaxing weekend there.

Most of the October days I've spent in San Francisco have been fairly chilly, but this particular weekend was perfectly sunny and mild. We exulted in the opportunity to walk as much as possible.

It had been suggested to my Dearest Companion that we visit the San Francisco Art Exchange, a gallery that was showing photographs of famous musicians from Sinatra to the Stones. Under normal circumstances, neither of us would have cared about seeing pictures of aging rockers in their glory days, but we decided to honor her friend's recommendation by popping in to take a look. The curator of the collection asked if we were in town for the festival, and upon finding out that I worked with Emmylou, he took us under his wing and gave us the Cook's tour.

Name-dropping has its perks.

In an off-limits room, we were given a glimpse of rare portraits of Elton John, Mick Jagger, and the Beatles. The curator explained that these prints were printed from the original negatives in limited runs, and the price tags were commensurate with their rarity.

The most captivating photograph was of Frank Sinatra tying his tie backstage, with a look of fatigue and weariness. He didn't seem to be enthusiastic about having done it "his way." It wasn't a flattering picture, but it was magnetic and telling, giving credence to the idea that when photographers take one's picture, they are stealing one's essence. Frank's vacant blue eyes looked like his soul had been captured one too many times.

We crossed the street and entered the Weinstein Gallery, quite by chance, where a showing of Robert Kipniss prints was premiering. Fantastic prints, painstakingly constructed, revealed not only the stark imagery of autumn, but also the dedication of an artist to finding perfection, beauty, and balance.

The curator of this gallery was a twenty-something young man, who knew his stuff. His enthusiasm was unbridled, and while we knew he hoped to find customers in us, it was apparent that he truly wanted us to be enlightened about Robert Kipniss's work.

Embracing us as eager students, our young teacher was more than delighted to dispense knowledge, explaining the painstaking print-making process, which involved carving a negative image onto several sets of stones.

We left with our heads full of crisp, floating autumn leaves, tree limbs emerging from blackness, taking root in the creative soil of two people who like to paint.

From the galleries on Geary Street, we walked over to Chinatown to the Red Blossom Tea Company, another recommendation. Our host was another twenty-something man, named Peter, whose family owned the business.

He stood with us at a wall of shelves on which hundreds of urns sat, full of fresh tea.

When my companion disclosed her taste for chai tea, Peter was diplomatically dismissive. We were informed that teas such as chai were low on the food chain of tea, and he compared them to cheap wine.

In moments like these, the "Southern" in my Southern Born Woman blooms like a fragrant rose, undeniable and undismissable.

"Well," she said wryly, "can you show me a tea that you can respect?"

Caught in airs, Peter broke into a smile.

She had him, as she often has had me.

He apologized and offered us a seat at a small table, where he methodically prepared tea. The ritual was calming and beautiful. As he brewed several different pots for us, he spoke of the origins of tea, taking great pleasure in dispensing knowledge to eager students.

Later in the evening, dining on paella and a good bottle of red zinfandel at the Hayes Street Grill, we noted the thread of passion that was woven from the photo gallery, to the print gallery, and finally the tearoom. How wonderful to have encountered people whose vocations had relevance and connection to things that they were passionate about.

"I'm not interested in what you're against," she often says. "Tell me what you're for."

Amen.

The next day, we decided to seek out a place of worship. We found Trinity Episcopal Church nearby and walked over. It was a grand place, but a sign on the door pointed us away from the sanctuary, and toward a small chapel.

Apprehensive about the follow-through, we poked our heads in for a look, and were immediately ushered up to the second row. We were probably twenty-five minutes late, arriving as congregants were exchanging the Peace.

Too late to turn back now.

The parishioners seemed to be from two groups, gay and octogenarian, with a few homeless people, and one exceedingly handsome young man and woman thrown in for good measure. Token heteros, I assumed, provincially.

Many were there with dogs and cats, and we realized that we had probably just missed the Blessing of the Animals.

On our left flank, not three feet away, sat a small choir, who rose for the offertory.

I'll give them an A for effort.

The basses and tenors were everything one would expect from a choir in San Francisco. But the altos and sopranos, all very old women, warbled with vibratos that felt like the tremorous prelude to an earthquake.

It was like being at a mother-son banquet for a gay men's chorus. Lapdogs welcome.

As we moved into the Communion part of the service, the odd little band of priests and acolytes began vigorously making preparations. The priest in charge was British, which made things feel properly Anglican. And God knows I'm all ears when it comes to an English accent.

But at some point, I tuned out, gazing about at the interesting group of worshippers. I was transfixed by an older, homeless man, who seemed blind, or perhaps blind drunk. I wondered about his story, making assumptions that probably had no basis in reality.

It was in this moment of daydreaming that I didn't see the other priest, a sixtyish woman, fall over. There was so little commotion, as if this was part of the service, perhaps a very radical form of genuflection, that I didn't even notice it. My Southern Born Supplicant, however, did notice, and wisely waited to tell me after the service.

It was a small act of kindness, God Almighty blinding me in that moment of unholy disruption, so that I wouldn't lock eyes with my woman and fall together into a spasm of laughter.

The service ended, and we left all smiles. It was one of the oddest church experiences we'd ever had, not life-changing, not particularly inspiring, but in its own way, it was lovely in its life-affirming kookiness.

I wonder how that English priest feels about his crazy little flock. Maybe he feels the same way Jesus feels about His crazy little flock.

Some Sunday mornings, I find myself sitting in a side pew at Christ Church Cathedral in Nashville. It's a vast room compared to Trinity Church's chapel out in San Francisco. I look around me and take note of the society types, the young couples, the widows, and even a few homeless, as is the case with most downtown churches. I notice, with a particular amount of warmth, quite a few gay couples sitting together, reciting the Creed, kneeling for prayers, and finally bringing the chalice to their mouths to receive the gift of God Almighty's passion.

I think of my gay friends who have tried everything to become ungay, like Brian, the former Seventh Day Adventist pastor, who has been through every antigay therapy known to man. Or Chris, the Christian rock fan who goes to a very Jesus-y church in Los Angeles that is a primarily LGBT congregation.

My friend Steve Hindalong played a concert at Chris's church in LA a while ago. Taken aback at the love these outcasts of Christendom had for Christ, Steve asked them why on earth they would still identify with Christianity.

They answered that they were compelled to love Christ; the "one true myth," as C. S. Lewis calls the love of Jesus, was a truth they couldn't repudiate, even in the face of rejection by many of Christ's followers.

And by some miracle, they found each other under God Almighty's motherly wings.

Get grace where you can find it, y'all.

I am weary of a phrase many Evangelicals have beaten into the ground: Love the sinner; hate the sin. As my friend Mark says, "Hate your own damn sin."

We can talk till the cows come home about every person being welcome in church, but this is an untruth of Evangelicalism. If you are gay, my friends, you are not welcome in their churches. So insistent are they on hating your sin that they don't have the time or the inclination to hate their own sins of pride, hate, gluttony, lying, misogyny, lust, and a list of isms too long to write down here.

I think I'd rather find myself in the company of displaced persons and lapdogs.

The next time my Southern Born Woman and I visit San Francisco, we'll seek out that little church again. And maybe once again the Body of Christ will bring us a good laugh.

29

Deluge

The flood came slyly, soothing my ears with its rainy, new age soundtrack tempting me to crawl back into bed on a Saturday morning and curl up with *London*, a book I'd been reading by Edward Rutherfurd. The gentle, steady beat of raindrops on my roof seemed an apt soundtrack for a book in which rain is a commonplace occurrence.

It had been a sad enough week, and like Stevie Ray Vaughn once sang, the sky was crying, perhaps for the two suicides that had rocked our town within days of each other.

One was a schoolmate of my daughter Maddy's, who had driven to the highest bridge in these parts, the Natchez Trace Bridge, which sits high above Highway 96 near Franklin, Tennessee. I guess the fear of living fueled whatever bravery was required for her to make the 155-foot leap to her end.

A few days later, a guitarist friend was having a conversation with his parents at his Franklin home. He casually went down into his basement and hanged himself. Will, as I remember him, had always been troubled. A few days after his death, a mutual friend and I noted that we'd both been shocked but not surprised.

The Kyrie was at the forefront of my mind, even before the deluge crept down the Cumberland. Lord, have mercy.

While I made a pot of coffee, the rain started seeping through the same old spot on the ceiling near my chimney.

It was the weekend, and I had work to do. Dennis Holt had come over to play drums on some music I'd recorded. As a rule, I like to record drums first and let the other instruments fall in line with their rhythm, but I had something I'd recorded "live" in my basement with John Paul White, a most passionate singer, who can croon, soar, twang, or roar. We had recorded what we call a "Guitar Vocal" version of the song, and I couldn't leave well enough alone. I decided it needed some buttressing, so I brought in Dennis.

If Dennis were a doctor, he'd manage to find the pulse of a corpse, so keen is his ear. I'll often bring him in and have him play on a haphazard recording, needing the cohesion, camouflage, and excitement his drumming can bring.

I like living in this community of musicians, who can drop everything and show up thirty minutes after an idea has been spawned. In no time, Dennis delivered the elements that had seemed lacking in the original recording.

When he left, it was raining pretty hard. A few minutes passed, and I continued working on the music. Dennis called and began talking about high water on Crockett Road and asking about alternative routes back to town. I sent him up to Concord Road and then shut my computer down, showered, and headed north. I was thinking my Southern Born Woman and I would enjoy the cozy sound of rain on the windows while reading a book we'd started.

Also, we had some tasks that needed doing in preparation for the debut of her play *Jezebel's Got the Blues and Other Works of Imagination*, so I sure didn't want to be stuck in the sticks. I was ready for an afternoon of working together, and of enjoying her company.

As I drove, I checked in with my daughter Kate, to see where she was and if she had shelter. She was working her checkout job at Target, and couldn't talk, so I left a message asking to be informed of her whereabouts once work let out.

About a mile from the interstate, Concord Road was underwater, and people were turning around. I took a right on Wilson Pike, a little two-lane road that crosses several streams on its way north. I'm a determined guy, and until a door slams in my face, I'll assume it's open. That character trait usually serves me well; not always, but usually.

Sure enough, I wasn't a mile up Wilson Pike when the low-riding Lincoln in front of me slowed down and surveyed the submerged road. It didn't look so bad to me, and I was feeling impatient. The Lincoln lurched forward and made it across the brook with me in tow.

I thought, *This is nothing*. That kind of thinking relates to yet another character trait, and perhaps that one has served me well, too. Not always, but usually.

The drive was oddly beautiful, surrounded by lush lawns and trees, but muddy waters continued to rise. Near the end of Wilson Pike, I came to a wide river burying all trace of the roadway. I waited as a southbound sedan tested the waters and passed me, water rolling from its wheel wells. Giving my car some gas, I faced the flood and plowed through, exactly where the southbound car had come from, while oncoming traffic waited to see what would become of me. I could feel the water splashing against the fenders, and pushing against my tires, but I made my way through, pumping my brakes once across.

Moments later, I was in Brentwood proper, out of the woods. I drove the remaining eight miles to my Dearest Companion's without incident.

She greeted me with a smile and a hug, and we chatted about her paintings and details of performing *Jezebel*. I was to provide the background music with my old National guitar and a slide, moaning the blues as actors gave voice to her musings about some troubled Old Testament characters, Jonah, Noah, Lot's wife, and others.

She asked for details about Will, and I gave her what sketchy information I'd been given. We wondered about his ex-wife and their sons, and talked about the impossible sadness of a funeral service when someone passes on in this manner, bequeathing to the survivors *the gift that keeps on giving*.

We worked for a while on her project, experimenting with canvas, paper, acrylic paint, and other media, then drove a few blocks away to a showing of paintings of trees by her friend Mindy. Little did we know that trees were falling fast at Radnor Lake, one of our favorite walking places. Nor did we know that the same was happening at other parks in our fair city.

We had no idea that there were neighborhoods being submerged by the overflowing Cumberland and Harpeth rivers, or that a grass-roots rescue effort would soon be under way. At Symphony Hall, the massive pipe organ was taking a beating, while the concert Steinway grand piano was being twisted, warped, and mangled.

Over at Soundcheck, where I used to keep my Hammond organ, and where many of Nashville's musicians rehearse and store their gear, the Cumberland was rising. Eventually the uncontained river would destroy over a thousand instruments, including priceless vintage guitars owned by Vince Gill, Keith Urban, and other fine musicians.

The Grand Ole Opry was underwater, but the Ryman Auditorium, the Mother Church of Country Music, was on high ground, for the moment at least.

Meanwhile, my Southern Born Woman and I huddled under a wide umbrella and walked up Belmont Boulevard to PM restaurant. We ordered our food and watched the TV overhead, with its sobering news, she eating sushi, and I eating a wasabi cheeseburger. If PM restaurant isn't washed away one day soon, try their cheeseburger; it's the best in Nashville.

Kate called in tears, wondering where to go from Target. I suggested she drive to our friend Derri's, who lives nearby. He was ready for her, as is the way of Nashville in crisis. It wasn't the first time our family had been scattered across town in bad weather. A small snowstorm has found my kids stranded at friends' homes.) Instead, she hightailed it to my place, which was a blessing in disguise. My basement was slightly wet, and she dutifully unplugged electrical gear and moved instruments to the living room.

Maddy was stuck at Kate's apartment, getting to be the little sister of Kate's roommates, thoroughly enjoying her independence, yet wondering when she'd get to go home.

Over the next twenty-four hours, we heard rumors and news of homes being damaged, and even a few lives being lost. My Southern Born Woman discovered three feet of southbound water in her basement, destroying her furnace and her water heater, but in light of what was going on elsewhere, she was grateful.

Eventually, I was able to reach Maddy and drive her back to my place. We passed the YMCA, where cars were completely covered by water. My neighborhood was untouched, perched as it is on high ground.

The next few days, the rest of the world didn't seem to be engaged with what is now being called the Thousand Year Flood. The only reason my family, scattered from Seattle to Ireland, knew anything was that I'd sent them pictures.

In the meantime, the Volunteer State lived up to its name. People with boats appeared on streets and rescued old-timers and newlyweds. Entire neighborhoods came together and gathered up the debris in the flood's wake, stacking sidewalks high with sofas, televisions, and miles of carpet.

Some people lost all possessions, only to find out that they had no flood insurance. I know of no reports of looting or gouging. I only know of a friend with a boat cruising up and down Sawyer Brown Road, searching for loved ones of strangers, ferrying helpless folks across a river that didn't exist the day before. I only know of songwriters and bands performing benefits, and tacos being delivered to volunteers who worked waist deep in rank basements, dismantling what the deluge had left behind, before any rebuilding would be possible.

They held Will's funeral in Alabama, where he'd grown up. It was packed with Nashvillians, but all the Volunteers in Tennessee couldn't corral the deluge he'd left his children swimming in. What can you say at the funeral of someone who takes his or her life? I wanted to say, "Will, are you happy now?"

I imagine he is.

There are some changes that come with no explanation or warning from Mother Nature. The "Act of God" clause in insurance policies has always miffed me; why blame God? Who's to say who sends the sunshine or the rain? When we need the rain, we thank God when it arrives, as we do when the sun relieves the dreary weather. But what of the Thousand Year Flood? I think all God has to do with it is in the hands of those who pull people to safety, who make sandwiches for workers, who clean out the debris, and who brush fingers across each other's brow, and whisper, *It's gonna be all right*.

30

In the Wake of the Deluge

Sometimes I wonder if the people who come up with names for neighborhoods, apartment complexes, streets, and parks should be required to take a course in literary aesthetics. I think zoning boards should prohibit stupid names.

For example, my old neighborhood is called Raintree Forest, which sounds to me like a feminine hygiene product. To my knowledge, there's no such thing as a "raintree." I'm sure of it because the spellcheck on my computer keeps highlighting the word in red.

Here in Tennessee, and perhaps in America in general, there is a fixation on naming suburban developments after English towns and villages. Having traveled the U.K. many times, I know something about the real places that suburban planners steal names from, and often they are not as quaint in reality as one might think. Have you ever been to Sheffield, England? If you had, you might not name your neighborhood after it. That being said, I had the best Indian meal of my life in the city of Sheffield.

When E and I separated, I moved into an apartment complex called the Enclave. Given the isolation one feels in the throes of a marriage dissolving, the complex was aptly named. Yet, the solitude I experienced emptied me in a way that allowed my soul to make room for the love that would come by way of friends, strangers, my children, and Spirit.

My two-bedroom place was pathetically empty—a bed in my room, and two beds in the other for my daughters. They were alarmed by the bare bones, but I liked it. The one luxury we had was a television sitting on a small wooden box.

I put an easel in the dining area and started painting again. I had stopped painting during the first months of my twenty-five-year marriage, and now felt myself being pulled back into what had been a contemplative exercise.

When the girls visited, we'd eat on the floor in the living room, where I would lay towels in case there was an accident involving food. I tried to make light of the situation by comparing it to the family camping trips we'd enjoyed in years past, but it didn't lessen my daughters' concern that my fortunes had truly gone south. I had no idea how alarmed they actually were until they told me several years later.

Most nights, after going to sleep, I would wake up drenched in sweat, starting at 1:00 a.m., and continuing till about five or six, until I finally couldn't take anymore. I would rise and go for a walk, but the neighborhood surrounding the Enclave wasn't much of a walker's paradise, so eventually, I started using the treadmill in the gym of the Enclave's clubhouse.

My isolation and restless nights drove me to exercising, and before I knew it, I had dropped forty or fifty pounds, power-walking two miles early every morning. Since I was already up, I now had a good ninety minutes before I needed to pick the girls up at E's for school. I discovered that my church, St. Bartholomew's Episcopal, had a morning prayer service at seven, so following my power-walk and shower, I'd head for the pews.

There were usually only three or four of us in those early morning hours, huddled in the first two pews, the sanctuary dimly lit, cold, and quiet. Led by Randy and Cathy, we would quietly work our way through prayers, Creeds, and scripture readings. I remember most of these mornings as rainy spring days that served as a metaphor for my journey, rainy with a slight chance of resurrection.

Randy, who would eventually become a full-fledged priest, had been someone I'd run from in the past. He had seemed a little too flaky to me, and was "Charismatic," like a lot of the crazies of my past who had attached themselves to me like barnacles to a boat's hull. This boat would *come about*, or turn around, when it saw Randy coming.

Now it was on the rocks.

Once he told me, "The Lord's been talking to me about you. Don't worry, most of it's good."

I started building a wall right there and then, and told him I had no interest in what the Lord was telling him. And I truly didn't.

The first time I attended morning prayers, the irony of redemption greeted me in the form of Randy's hug. I was informed by our past, yet I felt strangely safe, and sensed that one or both of us had changed.

I became a morning prayer regular for that short yet excruciatingly painful period of my life. Randy and Cathy would embrace me upon arrival, and upon intoning the words "Peace be with you" at the service's end.

One day, I asked him if he remembered what God had said to him back when I had started building my wall. He said, "Oh, that? That was just crazy talk!"

Those days of early morning power-walks and prayers got me through the early pain of divorce. Sometimes, departing from the church in my old Mercedes, I would experience a deluge of tears. My therapist told me my heart was thawing out and making room for love, but I just wanted to dam up the flood and get on with living.

Other times, I'd have a remembrance of a painful event that I had shoved to some dark corner of my memory. I would be taken by surprise, ambushed by a rusty, jagged remark. Often, I would be haunted by the unknown price my kids would pay for my decision to leave their mother. Of course, that is still a viable concern.

Of those tear-stained days, what I remember most is the centering experience of being in a house of God Almighty in the early hours, intoning ancient prayers in the hope that I wouldn't completely lose my way.

A few months passed, and the gavel came down, and the divorce was final.

I continued my exercising, but eventually, morning prayers fell by the wayside.

Six years passed. Water under the bridge. Water over the bridge.

In the wake of the Nashville flood, I had a personal awakening. I had no personal losses, as did so many other Nashvillians, but those deep waters brought with them a mystical effect on my life. Seeing the mini-islands that the flood created, I faced a reality check. How like an island was I willing to become? How willing was I to isolate from my daughters, my friends, and my Dearest Companion?

There were patterns of behavior that might isolate me if I continued them. No, there was nothing scandalous, nothing extraordinary, but I was easily lured into feelings of self-entitlement.

Looking around at the massive damage the flood brought to Tennessee, and seeing people's homes and lives put in disarray, I found myself with a crowbar and a hammer at the homes of a few friends whose places had been badly damaged. I was reminded of how good I had it, and of how blessed I was in friends, family, love, and work.

Witnessing the generous spirit unique to Middle Tennessee, and exhilarated by the experience of volunteering, even in the most basic of ways, I was reminded that this is how we're supposed to live *all the time*, not just while in dire straits.

The flood had swept across my eyes, and cleared my vision, and revealed the island I might be unto myself, if I didn't find my center.

So, on a Tuesday morning, six years, to the day, after the day of my divorce, I walked into a small neighborhood church at 7:00 a.m. and bent my knee before God Almighty, hoping I'd find myself surrounded and grounded by Spirit in the wake of the deluge.

31

Getting Down with the Joneses

It was a miracle when E and I moved into our first house. My parents gave us the seventy-five-hundred-dollar down payment on what seemed like a lot of money at the time—forty-five thousand dollars in 1984. Our little log cabin on Nebraska Avenue in Nashville's Sylvan Park was funky and warped, but cozy enough. It was small, too, but we enjoyed it.

From Sylvan Park we followed several friends and families out to Bellevue, on the western edge of Nashville. Wayne and Fran Kirkpatrick lived a street away, which led to a lifelong friendship with them, as well as a musical relationship with Wayne. A few hillsides away lived Bonnie Keen, who was and remains one of my Dearest Companion's dearest companions.

It was in that happy little Bellevue home that we received our two daughters, but we weren't there long enough for them to have much memory of it.

Next came a move to Green Hills, a popular Nashville neighborhood, which gave us a fine elementary school and a coffee shop I could walk to every morning. The home was a large, brick cottage with an English appearance about it. It had character, along with a damp basement, cracking plaster, and beautiful hardwood floors.

That house stood witness to a marriage that was starting to implode, and it was the site of our attempt to try to save "us."

Yet the happy times outshone the sad moments, and if my children are sentimental about any place they've lived, it is that Green Hills house.

But greener hills, or so they seemed, called.

I found a McMansion in boring Brentwood, with something as rare as a basement in Tennessee. Its high ceilings would give me a perfect recording environment, and the housing division would provide E with a tennis court, and the kids with a community pool and good schools.

People were shocked and disappointed when we made the move. One friend decried our situation, saying, "You're going to live among the Republicans!"

And so it came to pass.

The Land Rover and the Mercedes sat proudly in the driveway. The piano teacher showed up on Tuesdays. The pool key hung on the back of the laundry door. The neighborhood association sent polite warnings about keeping things uniform, along with invitations to cocktail parties.

Apart from Leon, a friendly man with a green thumb, we never met our neighbors, most of whom were nine-to-fivers who drove through yawning garage doors at the end of the day, only to be seen on weekends, tending to lawns and gas grills.

The mirage of better schools and of a better life dissipated into a reality that included finding a private school to accommodate my daughters' needs, which had been so well met in Nashville's school system.

The Raintree Forest neighborhood was pleasant, but not vibrant. The house was big and beautiful, but it lacked character. It had no history other than the sad story we would bequeath to its walls.

After the split, which I've written about elsewhere, E was smart enough to seek out humbler digs. I felt like selling the house would bring one change too many for the kids' already rocking world. I wound up staying in the big house, as it were, and indeed the sprawling four-thousand-foot edifice was more of a prison than a home. I went through seasons of indecision about staying or selling, and when I finally decided to let go, the property had lost an amazing amount of value.

My real estate agent gave me the bad news. "You'll need to short sell," she said. Suddenly, the trajectory of an adulthood of buying, selling, and upward mobility brought me to the bottom. Years ago, when we bought our first home, we had barely imagined being homeowners. Twenty-seven years later, I hadn't imagined a day coming when I would once again be a renter.

In the process of selling, I received a notice from a collections attorney whose name was so ridiculously close to the word "cheater" that I had to laugh. This particular cheater was trying to saddle me with thousands of dollars in attorney fees that didn't add up. "Cheater" was well-known in the real estate and banking community, and no one was arguing with the uncanniness of his surname. Somehow, I was led to a person who helped me to get out from under the shadow of a lawsuit, but I still shudder at the precariousness of the situation.

A contract on my home finally materialized, and I started looking around for a new place to live. The first place I looked at had its possibilities. It was about two-thirds the size of my first house in Sylvan Park, and the rent was three times its mortgage payment.

I continued looking, and while I felt good about the possibility of being debt-free, and tried to embrace the idea of starting over, the American Dream's indelible thumbprint had pressed long and hard into my psyche. I felt overwhelmed by what I didn't know, and thought of how impressive my stock portfolio *wasn't*.

In the meantime, friends from Colorado had signed me up for a daily quotation from a monk named Richard Rohr. Every day, it seemed as if Richard were reminding me that ownership was a myth and that I might as well let go of *everything*. I'd go to sleep at night and wonder if, like Jesus, I would wind up with a rock for a pillow. This wasn't what I'd signed up for, but in my heart I knew that the American Dream had never been *my* dream.

My Southern Born Woman was encouraging and sweet, affirming who I was, not what I'd accomplished, yet hopeful that my aspirations and efforts at rebuilding my material life would pay off.

One afternoon after leaving her place, I couldn't find my prescription Ray-Ban Wayfarers, the nicest sunglasses I've ever owned. Without flinching, I had sold vintage guitars that meant the world to me, rare old Ludwig drums that I'd never see the likes of again, and even the beautiful piano I'd written a few bona fide hit songs on, but somehow losing those replaceable Ray-Bans was a sad thing to me. They'd been around the world with me, and (let's face it) gave me some needed cool factor in the face of my uncool circumstances.

I drove as the sun sank low, and I pulled the visor down and squinted. *I'm in the middle of a short sale, and I'm sad about my sunglasses! What's wrong with this picture?*

As is often the case with lost key rings and glasses, they turned up a few hours later under the passenger seat of my car. I was overjoyed, frankly. They're prescription glasses—i.e., expensive—and they only work for me. Anyone who finds them, assuming I lose them again, will just get a headache from wearing them. (But they will look cool.)

A few days later, my Dearest Companion and I walked to the Belcourt Theater, a landmark in Nashville's Hillsboro Village. We watched *Of Gods and Men*, a beautiful film about the Martyrs of Atlas, seven monks who were killed in Algeria in 1996.

The portrayal of their life of simplicity, and the wholesome affection these brothers had for each other, was almost disturbing in its beauty. In contrast to my downsizing from four thousand square feet to perhaps fifteen hundred, here were men living in small cells, silently going about their menial tasks, and ministering to the small Muslim community with medical aid and other comforts.

In one beautiful scene, one of the brothers walks into the kitchen where the others are waiting to eat. He opens two bottles of red wine and blasts Tchaikovsky's *Swan Lake* on a cassette player. The joy of communion, of sharing a common cup, elicits laughter and beaming smiles from brother to brother, yet as the music gains intensity, tears of joy mingle with tears of loss, tears of the inevitable, ultimate Letting Go.

I'm writing these words midway through Lent, at which time I've chosen to *let go* of alcohol, fried food, and sugar. I've never enjoyed the burn of club soda as much as in the last few weeks. I've never enjoyed a "feast day" (Sundays or holy days) as much as in this particular Lent, when a taste of Bushmill's isn't taken for granted, but savored and sipped and contemplated.

There are times when I've flat-out given up Lent for Lent. Let's face it; it's a miracle that I have anything to do with "organized religion" after all the years of punching the clock in Sunday school, youth group, Wednesday night church, and a childhood of Sundays bereft of *The Wizard of Oz* and *The Wonderful World of Disney*, whose hours of broadcast coincided with Sunday evening services.

This year, I'm embracing Lent like it's a brother monk come to teach me something of the Spirit. There's a sensitivity that the self-imposed lacking has rewarded me with. Tomorrow, I might be my brash, carpetbagger self, but today, I'm listening. I'm remembering my moonless night of the soul. In my darkest hour of letting go, my Dearest Companion spoke wisely. "Baby, you're going through a death, and what better time than Lent? Soon enough, Easter will be here."

I'm looking forward to Easter, at which time I am going to get sick on a few morsels of chocolate. I'm going to take my Dearest Companion to the park before the sun comes up, and we will spread a

Tennessee Titans blanket on the damp grass that overlooks a wide field, with a hilly backdrop, which will slowly glow blue to green to orange to yellow as we ponder the Resurrection of Jesus, and the power tangled up with letting go.

I'll fire up the Coleman stove (which I guess I won't be letting go of), and I'll cook bacon and eggs over its blue flame while she reads me the *Times* or Flannery O'Connor, or better yet, a poem of her own. Who knows, maybe we'll bring the Book of Common Prayer just to organize things a bit. Maybe I'll be done with letting go, for a season, and no doubt, we'll lift a glass of something strong to our broken stories, while we're thinking of Resurrection.

And perhaps for a moment, we will bask in the joy of love and communion, and of not keeping up with the Joneses, while a tear falls, unseen behind my sunglasses.

32

Tequila Sunset

Like a failing marriage, its walls were cracked from a weak foundation. It had lost value and was, for me, a losing proposition.

The good news was that I had a buyer for my home. I was ready to be out of an edifice that had been anything but edifying. It was the site of my marriage falling apart, and around its perimeter sinkholes were appearing and evergreens were dying.

The bad news was the timing of the sale. The week before closing, I was in Norway having my fifty-ninth birthday. Actually, I was there for a pair of Emmylou concerts, but it sounds sophisticated to say that I spent my birthday in Oslo.

The dollar was as weak as a cup of Cracker Barrel coffee, and it was nigh unto impossible to find an affordable meal to ring in my last year of fifties-hood. The gin and tonic our drummer Bryan bought me cost twenty-two dollars.

Note to self, celebrate next birthday in America.

I returned to the big house from Norway on the Monday evening before closing. I had three days in which to vacate the premises. Having already packed some things, I was overly optimistic about my ability to get the job done.

So, on Tuesday I began arduously packing my possessions up, and discarding as much of what wasn't "life" as I possibly could. It was difficult work, combing through boxes that hadn't been unpacked since we'd moved in ten years before.

I had a box set aside for E, as I knew I'd be unearthing artifacts that might interest her. It had been a while since my garage-cleaning episode, wherein I'd discovered a part of our life that I'd forgotten, but this time I combed through happier days without time for pondering.

The garage held the cache of trash whose presence wouldn't be missed in my next living space. I donned a dust mask and spent hours sorting and deciding.

The easiest task was determining what to give to charity; if I couldn't sell it on the Internet, I would take the writeoff and let someone else carry it off. Tools, ladders, furniture, bicycles, and old videos were carted off by two men from Goodwill.

A few friends dropped in at various hours to give some muscle to my madness, and we put all the heavy items into a storage pod. I noted that one of these good men had helped me move in two other Nashville moves. Another had helped me move into my temporary digs during the early days of my split.

While I'd been in Norway, a songwriter pal, Cindy Morgan, came over and wrapped all my glassware and kitchen accoutrements. El Paso, a fellow chile relleno connoisseur, appeared in my front hall and offered to box up the endless ephemera of my man cave.

That night, my Dearest Companion invited me to dinner with her parents, who had just driven in from Texas, and her three kids, all of them gathered in Nashville to celebrate her son's wedding. He and his fiancée had planned a simple yet elegant, family-only affair for later in the week, and they had just arrived in time for our meal.

We had a fine time, feasting on her delectable cooking, drinking red zinfandel, and eventually retiring to her living room where all three children serenaded us with original songs. That's not necessarily atypical of Nashville, a town teeming with musicians, but when it's your kids (or those of your Dearest Companion), it's that much more enjoyable.

I got home fairly late and spent a few hours dividing my possessions into "keep" and "throw" piles. Dawn arrived sooner than I'd hoped, and I rose early, working a little before one last recording session in my studio. Looking back, it's just crazy that I had booked the session, but it's what I do; I make my living playing on records, and in 2011, no one was turning down work.

My friend Lari came over and I played accordion and organ on a few tunes she was producing, wrapping up as a helper arrived in the form of Bryan Owings, the aforementioned gin and tonic buyer. We've toured the world together, and on this day, we were both a bit jet-lagged from our Norwegian trek, but there he was, lifting a sofa with me and encouraging me to keep a few items I was more than ready to hand off to the Goodwill fellows. I was too tired to argue with him.

Bret, a recording engineer who had seen my request for moving help on Facebook, showed up and began carefully packing all the studio gear and instruments. After a while Bryan left, and another songwriting buddy showed up to help with more heavy lifting.

You know who your friends are.

Wednesday night was the rehearsal dinner, hosted by my Dearest Companion at an East Nashville Mexican restaurant called the Rose Pepper. We feasted on deep-fried avocados and spicy entrees laced with chorizo and cilantro, washing it all down with pitchers of margaritas.

I drove the Texans back to their hotel and then returned to the nocturnal task of sorting and heaving until 3:00 a.m.

Thursday, the day of the wedding, I woke to do more sorting, but it was the heaving that my body was more inclined to do. I couldn't lift my head without becoming fiercely nauseated.

I was thinking of calling my realtor and telling her that there was no way I was going to be out of my house by Friday morning, when she walked in with her friend Rusty, and announced that she'd rented a U-Haul truck.

I lay prostrate on the floor, trying to articulate what needed to be left alone, what needed to be thrown, what needed to be put in the pod, and what needed to go on the truck, while unable to lift my eyes long enough to connect with the faces of the gracious angels come to my aid.

Rusty, whom I'd never met, knelt beside me and started speaking in tongues, and then prayed in English that God would heal me, and heal me quickly. I had been around plenty of "tongue-talkers" in my crazy days at Love Inn and in Christian music, and to my way of thinking, it's never seemed very sensible. But if tongue-talking was going to get rid of my nausea, I was all for it.

Suffice to say, God Almighty took plenty of time in getting back to Rusty about my illness.

Meanwhile, friends showed up and helped out, as I lay on the den floor between bouts of vomiting the antinausea medicine and the last night's tequila. So delirious was I that my collected visions of these good people—Wayne, Bret, Steve, Mark, and even my daughter Kate—are a blur.

Occasionally, I would test my sea legs to see if I could walk two feet without stupendously hurling. More than once, helpers leaped aside as I caromed through the halls toward the nearest sink.

It occurred to me that I needed to rent a storage unit for all the junk in the U-Haul, so I carefully got into my car, with an empty cup in hand (just in case), and drove to a storage place. Mickey, the woman who managed the storage place, was leading the way through the hot sun to show me what kind of unit I'd be renting when I began uncontrollably vomiting once again. I apologized and assured her that it wasn't a commentary on her business.

Discouraged, I signed on the dotted line and got into my car. Too weary to call my Dearest Companion, I started writing a text message, surrendering to the harsh fact that I wasn't going to be at the wedding, which would be occurring in less than two hours. I had been asked to sing a song for the bridal procession, and sadly realized that that honor was slipping away.

Halfway through the word "heartbroken" I stopped.

I feel better, I thought.

I was sorry not to give Rusty and his tongue-talking the credit for my feeling better, but after all the time God Almighty had taken in answering, I wasn't inclined to start singing hymns of praise. Mother Nature had taken her course, and fortunately Her schedule and the wedding were in close enough sync.

God Almighty nonetheless had provided good friends who provided a miracle of sorts by joining in the task of moving me out of a place that never felt like home.

Speeding back to the house, where a crew had continued working, I realized I might be a few minutes late, but I would indeed be at the nuptial celebration.

I quickly showered and shaved, brushed the hell out of my teeth, and dressed up in my Sunday best. Speeding up I-65, I called my Southern Born Woman and said I was running late, but not too late. Wise one that she is, she had implored her talented daughters to have something ready to sing, just in case.

Nothing goes without a hitch, and as soon as I arrived at the wedding chapel, I unpacked my guitar to find that its strings had been loosened to death for the flight back from Norway. Everyone waited quietly while I tuned. Tick tock...

And then I sang.

I don't even remember the song I sang. Even while singing it, I was somewhere else, caught up in the miracle that ninety minutes earlier, I'd been sick as a dog.

We all enjoyed a lovely private evening together watching two people attempt the thing that a few of us hadn't been successful at.

Marriage.

As I listened to their vows, I thought of the cycles of life. I thought of the happenstance that brings each of us into this old world, and I thought once again that, despite the circumstances of failure and accidents, I've never for a moment believed that anyone exists without God meaning for us *to be*.

I looked at this young man, full of grace and confidence, face shining with optimism, and I felt thankful for knowing him. I thought of his mother, my Dearest Companion, and her tireless love of her children.

Naturally, my musings led me to my own daughters, who are always with me, always in mind, always loved. I thought of the failed marriage that had brought my girls into the world, and the house of an errant dream, which seemed so culpable in my undoing, now left groaning and empty, save for the ghostly remnants of echoed unanswered prayer.

The vows were said, and I watched a tear grow in my Dearest Companion's left eye, until it spilled joyfully down the side of her face, marking a milestone in her journey.

I was emotionally full and physically empty. I'd spent a few days purging, quite literally, and now I was at a feast, and I might add, I had an amazing appetite.

Regarding my violent nausea, there's a part of me that feels like 'fessing up and admitting that I probably went one margarita over the line. But maybe the truth is, I was sick of a house that had given nothing back for all it had taken.

The cycles of our lives bring us sadness and goodness. They bring love and hate, forgiveness and unforgiveness, wealth and poverty. Life is a liturgy that is summed up in Christmases, Good Fridays, and Easters, lives, deaths, and resurrections, between which we make whatever we might of our desert pilgrimages and evergreen homecomings.

33

The Chick Upstairs, Part 2

So I moved into Werthan Mills, an old factory that has been turned into lofts. My place was three stories, wooden floors, old beams and brick. The starkness was luxuriously appropriate.

When I told Rob Grant my address was on Rosa Parks Boulevard, he wrote back and wryly said at least I'd have good bus service.

In the middle of June, I moved my stuff in, and immediately went on a long tour with Emmylou Harris and her Red Dirt Boys. Sleeping on the bus or in a hotel room, I would smile and think about my artist loft at Werthan Mills. I relished the thought of finally being out of suburban Brentwood, away from the McMansions, in a new place that had no carpets, no lawn, and no tennis moms.

I imagined writing, painting, recording, and relished the idea of waking in my loft bedroom above the rest of my new little world.

We had a short break in July, and I finally spent a night in my new digs. At about 6:00 a.m., my upstairs neighbor started seizing her day and mine. The sound of the hardwood floors and her high heels wasn't going to be muffled. I lay paralyzed in bed, staring at the wooden ceiling. I didn't realize that a person could walk so far in one little apartment, but she certainly paced as if she was heading somewhere.

I thought, *Damn, this isn't going to work.*

I was all too happy to get back on the road for another three weeks.

Driving back to Nashville from Newport, Rhode Island, I had plenty of time to think about creative things, but all I could do was dread coming home and listening to the footfalls of the chick upstairs. I could hear the still, small creak of her body shifting weight.

It was my Southern Born Woman who reminded me of what I'd written earlier about the Chick Upstairs. I was struck by how willing I am to allow God to speak to me through an annoying woodpecker, or a stranded horse, or a perfectly silent owl, but much less open when it comes to a human being.

It's easy to find the face of God in people we get along with, even better in people who get along with us.

Bassist Byron House, who is a devout Christian, refers to the bands he's played with as "assignments." "When I was on assignment with so and so" is his way of saying that God has him on this gig or that to be a light, and a bright light he is, loving and gentle-spirited, and a helluva bassist to boot.

Growing up Evangelical, I carry that mindset around, too. "This little light of mine, I'm gonna let it shine." To some Christians, everything a believer does is going to reflect on Jesus, so it better be good. Fair enough.

I like the idea of God having you where you're supposed to be, although I think it's more of a two-way street than the one-way variety my friend implies the Almighty has put us on. In my travels with Emmylou, I have seen some mighty bright lights shining, beckoning me to shine, too.

I've rarely experienced the kind of generosity our guitarist, Will, exhibits. Bryan's gracious manner, Chris's weighing of a word, and Rickie's sagelike wisdom all call me higher, and all remind me that you can't escape the Light of Christ; you just might be dumb enough to deny it.

The night we played in Central Park, a friend in the audience told me that Emmylou seemed like a priest presiding over a great

Eucharist. She does her work with such grace and authenticity even those of us onstage with her are moved during the performance.

When it comes to my lucky gig, the mystical assignment might have more to do with learning than teaching.

The tour came to an end, and I hauled my guitars and accordion back to the loft.

My first night "home" the chick upstairs paced until about three in the morning. For a few days, it rained footfalls. One morning, I woke up depressed, and wondered how I was going to make it in this new, noisy, uncarpeted environment.

I've never missed Brentwood, mind you. Suburbia is just not my cup of tea. But it had coddled me and lulled me into a trance in which I forgot how noisy the world really is.

One morning at seven, the footfalls came, and I decided to read something inspirational, remembering how brother woodpecker had called me to prayer back in suburbia. And I thought of waking early in Amman, Jordan, years ago, the sun barely peaking over dusky, squat buildings as a foreign song called Muslims to prayer from a nearby minaret. It was a magical wake-up call, nearly Pentecostal in its timbre, yet without emotion.

I forgave the noise because it was exotic. I embraced it as a part of the travel experience.

Then I got home and forgot that I was still on a journey.

I'm slowly waking up to the fact that it isn't about me. Truth is, I find God annoying as he carves away at the bark around whoever I am to become. When I damn his children, his creatures, his bright sun or his dark sky, it's really just another case of my taking his name in vain.

So I wrestle and wrestle. And maybe at 7:00 a.m. tomorrow, when the Chick Upstairs wakes me with those patent leathers, I'll try to bless her name.

34

Hearing Things

I've spent a lifetime listening to holy rollers saying, "God told me" this or that, but I've never had that kind of experience. There was a time I envied those who believe they've heard God's voice, as if I were missing out on a life-changing encounter.

But I am blessed with limited vision, skepticism, and education. I'm blessed not to walk under the inescapable weight of such cosmic responsibility. A crazed determination can follow such an experience, like building an ark or wearing a sandwich sign proclaiming black-and-white ultimatums like "Turn or burn!"

I prefer the filtered version of God's voice, as I prefer my whisky. Let the message age a while in a warm oak cask. My ears, worn down by the blues, smoothed by the rough edges of angular voices, listen with acquired wisdom, and a need to listen twice before interpreting.

It was my seventh Christmas as a single dad. The old traditions had given way to new. For instance, my Christmas now came a day early on the twenty-fourth, a nice compact holiday with my daughters which entailed opening stockings, having Swedish pancakes for breakfast, opening gifts, and watching *A Christmas Story*, and, if time permitted, *It's a Wonderful Life*. All this lazing about would lead to a dinner that had evolved with their taste buds, which currently were vegetarian. No more squeezing meat through a grinder into sausage casing, becoming korv, and no more Swedish meatballs.

Now the meal was my famous vegetarian shepherd's pie, which sounded Christmas-y enough, and, being garnished with lingonberries, brought back some of our old family flavor.

That first divorced Christmas was strange for all of us, and no doubt I compensated in the gift department, hoping to take the edge off the obvious, jingling all the way.

In the three years before my Southern Born Woman invited me to spend Christmas evening with her, I joined a friend and her country relatives for a southern Christmas lunch, and then spent the balance of Christmas alone. It wasn't as sad as it sounds, but it was quiet and different. I sat in a room whose walls looked like painted leather and strummed an old Gibson guitar while the fire crackled. Jimmy Stewart and Donna Reed embraced in hot passion, the TV mute, as I played no particular song.

Divorced Christmas number two found my girls and me flying, along with their mother, to my father's funeral in Rhode Island. He had died Thanksgiving weekend, but my mother had postponed the proceedings till December 26 so that the entire world could make plans to be there.

That was the year we lost Dad, and thus a large part of my mother.

So, Christmas number seven rolled around with a new set of parameters. The tradition of putting up the fake tree I'd bought on Divorced Christmas number one was gone—I'd given it to men of Goodwill when I moved out of the big Brentwood sprawl that housed the spirit of failure, the museum to the artifacts of another time.

Now I was in my downtown loft, with the chick upstairs constantly pacing, waking me every morning at precisely seven, walking back and forth across the twelve-foot span of my bedroom ceiling, until departing for work at 7:50. Presuming I wouldn't stay beyond my one-year lease, I hadn't even unpacked. Boxes sat unopened and taunted me with the punch line of my pending homelessness.

I thought of stringing lights across my little balcony, and thought of hanging ornaments around the kitchen and the living room, but I didn't know what boxes they were packed in.

I was painting with Jimmy Abegg on the twenty-third, and in the spirit of ridiculousness, we took scissors to cardboard and created a pair of pathetically wonderful Christmas trees.

Even so, the girls arrived on Christmas Eve *Eve*, gleeful and ready to busy themselves making gifts, as had been our agreement in this season of frugality. The dreadful economy brought with it inventiveness and a bountiful spirit of DIY. So, we sat in our private nooks, working away on simple gifts of affection—drawings, embroidered or painted ornaments, and words.

The next morning we began our day, and followed to the letter the menu I've written above, except that I had added blackberry pie to the mix. The cardboard tree stood lightless with our simple gifts spread 'neath its painted boughs.

It's a Wonderful Life was too long to squeeze into our schedule, so the girls opted for some holiday episodes of a cartoon called *King of the Hill*, which centers on the amusingly dull life of Texan Hank Hill, a propane salesman. That measure of dark humor is something of a trademark with my daughters and me. It's an inexplicable counterbalance to the wide-eyed wonder we can experience when considering the blessings of our life. I suppose cynicism can be a safeguard for those who've watched their families disassemble, or perhaps it's just a by-product of being a young American in the early twenty-first century.

Charles Dickens must have been rolling in his grave. But perhaps we were living out a most Dickensian of Christmases, having endured our losses while clinging to the essential core of Christ's birthday.

At 7:30, we headed off to Christmas Eve Mass at St. Bartholomew's Episcopal Church, where we had attended before the divorce, and where E was still a member. This had been part of our tradition as well, my showing up at the church I no longer attended, much to the delight of a few folks who wondered if I had somehow lost my way and rediscovered it on Christmas Eve, like Ebenezer Scrooge of old.

I sat with the girls, one dressed like a ragamuffin, the other dressed like a supermodel, three rows from the back. We saw a few familiar faces and exchanged smiles as the carols began floating toward Heaven.

I'm not much of a hymn singer, and if the Episcopalians have a lack, it's singable hymns; they somehow opt for melodies that are impossible to harmonize with unless you're an English choirboy or a castrato.

Christmas is an exception; they sing all the hits, and on this Christmas Eve I found myself singing "Angels We Have Heard on High" with gusto, my voice reminding me of my father's, his baritone having been passed down to me along with his baldness.

I always think of him when I sing hymns; I hear his voice in mine, just a plain and earnest sound, warm light through an old cornet, nothing remarkable but for the sound of faith.

Hearing the genetic link between my voice and my father's, I thought of Dad in that other world, and I choked on the morsel of grace lodged in the back of my throat. I heard him singing from beyond the grave, reminding me that the mercy of a good father has always been my lantern on the road home to the heart of God.

Moments later, I heard myself intoning the Nicene Creed, as my daughters stood near me, and I wondered if one day they might recite these things and remember my voice as I remember Dad's.

The scripture from Isaiah reminded me of something my Southern Born Woman had written about the prophet a while back in her play *Jezebel's Got the Blues and Other Works of Imagination*. She writes of Isaiah spanning the Old Testament and the New, being split by two paradigms, law and grace, not to mention being literally sawn in half.

I heard God's DNA coiled around her vocal cords, drawing me to drink from a deep well of holy water and confounding grace.

I related to her musings about God building a bridge between two worlds. I pondered the ancient scribe prophesying the story of Jesus' coming and his Incarnation...I thought about Jesus spanning two universes, His arms stretched across the chasm between mortality and immortality, closing the gap whose distance is immeasurable, yet contained within the finite longing of humanity.

My girls and I embraced during the Passing of the Peace, and I was acutely aware of the grace passing between our hearts. I can be as sentimental as the next man, but there was nothing sappy going on in this sacred moment. I was recognizing Jesus in the people whom I love and who love me so well.

By the service's end, I could barely speak.

I had heard God's voice.

God sounds like my father calmly singing.

God sounds like my daughters saying "Peace be with you."

God sounds like the silence in my Dearest Companion's graceful gaze, accepting, and embracing.

God sounds like the bold poetry that rolls off her elegant pen, daring me to believe that a bridge is being built in my heart from the Dead of Winter to the Light of Christmas.

God sounds like a rushing wave, lifting my boat from its lonely reef and carrying me Home.

APPENDIX

God on the Rocks: Music to Savor

The Choir: *The Loudest Sound Ever Heard*

Emmylou Harris: *Stumble Into Grace*

Mahalia Jackson: *Gospels, Spirituals & Hymns*

Blind Willie Johnson: *The Complete Blind Willie Johnson*

Phil Keaggy: "Sunday's Child"

Mat Kearney: *City of Black & White*

Phil Madeira: p.m.

Taj Mahal: *The Real Thing*

Mercyland: Hymns for the Rest of Us—Various Artists

Buddy Miller: *Midnight and Lonesome*

Shawn Mullins: "The Ghost of Johnny Cash" (from *Light You Up*)

Buddy Miles: *Them Changes*

Dave Perkins: *Pistol City Holiness*

Sister Rosetta Tharpe: *The Gospel of the Blues*

Nedra Talley Ross: "Be My Baby"

Author's Acknowledgments

It takes a village to make a book.

In the case of what you are holding in your hands, my friend Ian Cron suggested I call Kathryn Helmers, a literary agent with Creative Trust. I couldn't blame her for being reluctant to read an unpublished writer, but I am thankful that she not only read, but also became a champion of my writing. In the process, she has become my friend.

Kathryn drew me back into the orbit of Creative Trust, particularly Dan Raines and Jeanie Kaserman, with whom I'd worked years before. Where does the time go?

A party at the aforementioned Ian's house led to a connection with Wendy Grisham. Not long after that, Kathryn introduced Wendy to my book, which led to my signing with her publishing company Jericho Books. I am thankful to her and to Chelsea Apple, her assistant, for their tireless efforts in bringing this work to print.

My editor Adrienne Ingrum understood me from the moment we were introduced, and I can't thank her enough for the care that she brought to a process that I initially feared. Not to mention our mutual love of Taj Mahal. I look forward to working with her again.

I have never met Sean Devlin, but I appreciate his keen copyeditor's eye. I still don't know where to place a comma.

I had been a fan of Wayne Brezinka's artwork before I knew his name. Again, my gratitude to goes to Jericho for suggesting that my book be graced by Wayne's edgy, soulful art.

I am thankful for every character—stranger, creature, friend, and foe—that populates these pages.

Lori Quinn made a point to introduce me to several agents and publishers before I had even organized my stories into book form. I'm grateful for her early advocacy.

Wayne Kirkpatrick, my dear friend of many years, has a quiet but strong part in some of these stories, whether I mention him or not. He and his wife, Fran, are like family to me.

Jimmy Abegg, with whom I paint on a regular basis, inspires me with his artful life, and his belief in all things being possible.

Bryan Owings reminds me often about the importance of rhythm, food, and drink. Between beats, bites, and sips, he has given continual encouragement to "keep walkin'."

I am extremely grateful to both Emmylou Harris and Buddy Miller for allowing me to make music and friendship with them.

My road mates for the last few years have become like a second family, and our travels around the globe have given me much to be grateful for, and much to write about. They include Richard Battaglia, Maple Byrne, Chris Donohue, Emmylou Harris, Steve Hartley, Byron House, Will Kimbrough, Colin Linden, David Mann, Buddy Miller, Bryan Owings, Carolyn Rosenfeld, Rickie Simpkins, and Bernie Velluti. (Will suggested my inclusion of a playlist as a soundtrack for the book. He also taught me how to use a delay pedal.)

There are numerous musicians, roadies, engineers, and techs who've inspired me and collaborated with me over the past forty years. Some are mentioned in these pages, some are not. To all of them, I send my gratitude.

Thanks to Todd Robbins, Cindy Morgan, David Mansfield, Steve Hindalong, Amy Grant, Anthony and Michelle Aquilato, Rob and

Pat Grant, The Americana Music Association, www.writingcircle.org, and whoever brews the iced coffee at Crema in downtown Nashville.

I am acutely aware of Jonathan, Evan, and Rebecca Farnsworth's beautiful impact on my life.

Thanks and apologies go to my siblings, Annie and Dave. They've allowed me to see things as I see them, have offered up the occasional correction of facts, and more important, have loved their brother. I love them back.

I hope the stories make clear my great regard for E, and my gratitude for our journey.

My daughters, Kate and Maddy, are the greatest teachers I've ever had. They are also two great women. I love being their dad. It can't be easy being the children of someone who makes his living out of dreams. If anything, I hope my successes and failures teach them to dream well.

None of this would have happened if my Southern Born Woman hadn't suggested the idea of devoting one night a week in which we each read something we'd written to the other. It was she who heard these stories in their most raw form, and she who gave invaluable criticism and encouragement to me. In truth, I wrote this for her.

About the Author

Phil Madeira is a musician, songwriter, producer, and singer. He has performed or collaborated with many major recording artists, including Alison Krauss, Elvis Costello, Mat Kearney, Amy Grant, Garth Brooks, Buddy Miller, and The Civil Wars.

He is the recipient of the Dove Award for Best Country Song, the 2000 Best Keyboard Nammy (Nashville Music Awards), and a humanitarian award from ASCAP for composing a song that aided the response to the Ethiopian hunger crisis of the mid-eighties.

In addition to being a solo performer, Phil is a member of Emmylou Harris's band the Red Dirt Boys.

In 2012, he conceived and produced the highly acclaimed album *Mercyland: Hymns for the Rest of Us*, an anthology of inclusive spiritual music that features The Civil Wars, the Carolina Chocolate Drops, John Scofield, Emmylou Harris, Dan Tyminski, Amy Stroup, Cindy Morgan, the North Mississippi Allstars, Buddy Miller, Shawn Mullins, Mat Kearney, and himself.

He is the proud father of two adult daughters, and lives in Nashville, Tennessee.

God on the Rocks is his first book.

Learn more at www.philmadeira.com and philmadeira.blogspot .com.